A list of your author's books
are attached in the back of this book
for your inspection.

Preliminary notes from your author

It is now the year 2014.

I must tell you this book on love was my first attempt at submitting "a" published book of my rather long experiences, exposure and education on the subject. I cannot say it is comprised of my best literary skills since, at that time of writing, I had more to learn in the "art" of writing, but as I have read it in later years, I have experienced reminders of love potentials for which I do practice every opportunity I get and learn more from them to write better.

I kindly ask for your toleration in any inept descriptions I may have unperfectively stated at the time and absorb the content of which will serve you in many ways into your future of love and relationships. Thank you for participating in these mind stretching efforts. L.E.M.

OPEN THAT DOOR

Let Love Out and Let Love In

A Psychology of Love

Lloyd E. McIlveen

 www.trafford.com

North America & international
toll-free: 1 888 232 4444 (USA & Canada)
fax: 812 355 4082

Loving and being loved are really very simple if you have the knowledge or instinct; or both.

The subtitle "Let Love Out" may seem like losing a very high grade talent, but that is erroneous. The following scriptures reveal some of the endless wonders and deceptions of this magical and glorious kingdom of which everyone wants, beside money;—Love.

Do you believe you have it? You may be pleasantly surprised to discover you have more of these talents than you ever knew. If not, they are available.

Preface

There are many words describing a brief generalization or connection to the concept of love like affection, amorous, attachment, brotherhood, captivate, desire, dependency, devotion, embrace, emotion, enamored, fondling, fondness, goodwill, hugging, infatuation, intimate, kissing, liking, pleasure, sex, tenderness and many more.

There are etymological expressions in dictionaries and bookstores on linguistics science of language for one who is more analytically seeking extensive meaning pertaining to these words of love.

Where there are general and practical purposes of becoming more compatible and/or intimate with another living being, a little education of a few personal experiences by one or those who have already experienced the ups, downs, goods and not so goods of love may be helpful.

The following chapters may be a good source of gaining new perception of how to blend in to the world of love without having to stumble all the way through life and then realize it could have worked better another way.

Most people just do not have the time to study concepts and attitudes concerning love and many are not even aware they have endless choices pertaining to the rewards love has to offer.

Lets move on and wade through the crux of it all and prevent tripping on our mistakes which are usually prompted by our ignorant and/or deceptive perception.

Let's reprogram our outlook on love to eliminate the waste of emptyness concerning love. Let's fill our consciousness with love so that emptyness will no longer exist and love will prevail.

Contents

Chapter 1

Where Did It Start?

When a fish has fertile eggs, is there any love attached to this procreation procedure?

Since we humans don't understand fish language, the foregoing conclusion could be we just don't know. Lets look into it.

How about wolves or bears? They appear to be affectionate with each other, so it may be assumed there is love between them, or at least "our" perception of love.

There are also humans who have, at least what we believe, a superior form of language that assists our ability to understand one another by virtue of what we say or do. Is it because of this great understanding of what we think we have that influences us to believe our way of loving is omnipotent to other forms of life? It's a very debatable subject.

How about an ant? If this all powerful concept of love is so big, can it really exist in something so small as an ant or maybe even a microscopic parasite?

Well, we human beings appear, sometimes, to have everything all figured out and that love with all of it's complications, is limited to humans only as it may seem.

Bringing insects, animals, people or any other living being cell into the world requires first, of course, a sexual act of some kind. All species have their own approach and some form of intimacy must exist, so let us do a little historical retrospect.

According to science in the study of ancient history, we were all under water at one time, which may indicate all living cell beings were alike on Earth and had the same psychobiological makeup as far as affection and love are concerned. This may help answer the fish question of love.

Apparently, in the beginning, part of this psychobiological makeup was the sensation of what we now call emotion. That sensation influenced our ability to trust or fear.

So, whenever a living being is confronted with something pleasant like a friend, something required like eating or something unpleasant like an enemy, our emotions are immediately called to help decide, on a constant basis, if these friends, requirements or enemies are really what we believe they are.

Let's connect man's emotions to animal life and compare: Since man claims animal life is perpetrated by instinct only, he is contradicting the theory where all living beings were basically the same in the beginning, at least pertaining to emotions. Also, since love involves so many intellectual and psychorhythmic extrapolations, it would appear only man would be capable of such sophisticated intimacies.

Well, back to Earth's beginning again. If we were all basically made-up of the same stuff, suffice to say, all living creatures large or small would have been created with similar abilities in love emotion as well as sex for procreation.

Do smaller fish swim in schools because they have a particular esteem for the school? How about zebra? They run in packs. Is it because they are having a love affair with other zebra? Of course the answer is no to both the fish and the zebra. They do it to protect their hydes from preditors.

It's been said love is the strongest emotion among humans. If that's the case and all living beings are assertively and reactionarily similar, then all living creatures must possess the ability to love which substantiates "love" is the strongest emotion. Let us continue to search.

So, if early bug and animal life experienced intimate, sexual and family type feelings, they must have experienced feelings of love quite possibly like we humans tend to.

Now, if we can decide all this is somewhat true about all living creatures, then it seems fair to say love can be right near the top of the list as a universal strength and it isn't just a more recent evolutionary development.

The question is still there though. Is it the very strongest emotion?

So far, it's only high on the list of our emotional drives and reactions and might be shouted out loud by masses of humans with strong family and sexual needs to say it is at the very top.

Now, ask the question only humans can ask. That is, what is our strongest and most continuous emotional drive?

Answers, of course, are all interpreted a little differently be each individual. Here is one: Animals and insects alike all look for, number one, cover of one kind or another especially when they sleep.

Number two is sleep. They become weak and vulnerable to preditors with out it. Next is food and water. Without those, they become discontented, disoriented and weak.

Humans, just as the animals, insects and microscopic organism require basics of cover, sleep, food and water for resistance against various opportunists and illness.

The drive to acquire these fundamental necessities, for all living beings on Earth, appear relentless and very high on the list of basic requirements.

The indication here, looking into the past, is where the necessities mentioned above must be met or while these beings are deprived of them, the use of better judgment could fall victim to exploitation, opportunist influenced addiction or self-inflicted illness. The results may be highly instrumental in the deterioration of love and survival.

Moreover, most nonaffluent populations and especially the regimented (ants, communists, slaves) type would probably be somewhat less interested in the social activity of love and be more concerned about promoting and maintaining those basics of eating and sleeping etc. for just plain surviving in this life.

So, according to all the previously mentioned conjectures and looking at it from the bottom line, the strongest emotional drive with the highest priority in all living beings is the need to survive; especially in view of the possibility animals and insects live with similar tendencies and experiences.

Apparently the emotion and/or concept of love also dates back to the beginning of all living beings and has continued to gain what we humans often refer to as strength or popularity.

These strengths of love may or may not be as they seem. Evidence supports an appearance and possibility they have been competing with that very popular need to survive for hundreds of millenniums or longer.

Is love and sex competitive? Is it necessary to know if it is competitive? Well, just by virtue of the fact we have a comparison of love/sex to the survival aspects of living indicates there are two strongly motivated drives of struggle in and between the satisfaction of procreation and maintaining existence. These drives are power houses of reasoning behind almost all living beings. That could be enough to shake those questions loose for answers that may help us to realize all living beings didn't simply start in the beginning without some basis of reasoning.

Reasoning behind all this motivation is not merely intellectual either. It "is" the powerhouse of feeling throughout our bodies and minds which stimulates our neurons and vessels toward arriving at a direction of desire. This is body and mind working together.

That is where the answers of what, where and importance come together.

All drives of motivation through the almost incomprehensibly complicated process of mind occurs when one bends an elbow to eat. That's one of the easier manipulations of the mind and body. Imagine what happens when one must decide, for instance, to let loose of love and/or sex in exchange for a career, money or maybe even a position of just staying alive; which are only general examples.

These are the termoils and challenges that keeps living beings hungry for the security of survival and satisfied with the passion of lust.

No one knows yet exactly when small, medium and large beings came in on the scene of life on Earth, but one possibility exists almost for sure. There was romance of some kind or we wouldn't have such an overpopulated planet of all shapes and sizes.

So, the questions will probably always remain (just as "which came first, the chicken or the egg?"), which really came first, the safe haven for procreation or the romance? Maybe in the beginning it was romance, but how about now?

Whenever and whatever, the concept of living whoever or whatever goes back a long way into the past. Certainly, by now, the possibility lingers where we could "cash in" on all those experiences with a little effort.

What is more important and/or meaningful and where do we stand on these love/survival issues? Let us delve into explore and discover the paths of direction toward understanding our instinctual heritage a little better.

Chapter four deals more with the position and mystery of love. First, though, let's look into chapter two on qualifications of love.

Chapter 2

Qualifying For Love

The title does sound a little cold to think we may have been born without that ability and have to undergo extensive educational training on the subject, then take a test and be hopeful we passed it and finally have to stand in many different lines to experience giving or receiving that very popular feeling.

The possibility in the case of humans, a little or even more education on the subject of love per se in the school system would be favorable or even more beneficial toward sharing and/or receiving these somewhat wonderful, neurotic and grandiose feelings; especially of a long term and more sincere basis as young people mature. If that's the case, humans would as they enter their maturing years, probably acquire more patience and understanding concerning giving and receiving so the love experienced may be longer lasting, less misunderstood and more rewarding for themselves and others too.

Okay, teaching what love is all about may be limited to certain eras of time and it's any body's guess as to when that may occur. After all, it is a timeless and heavy subject.

However, the subject of love is wide open if society decides they want to expand on it to a more in depth manner through eliminating their crystallized beliefs and monitary attitudes which prevent more love to flow throughout nations of the world.

We must not think of getting something back to experience giving love or the giving part will only be an act like a stage show and like a stage show, the audience may applaud greatly, but they will be aware of the act being over and exit the theatre. The same may happen in a real scene.

All of we humans play games with each other one way or another like learning one's weaknesses to capitalize on them, taking unfair advantage of many people to find the right mate. Swindling money etc., etc.

Those are acts of deception for self-gain only. Nothing is given by the actors and only grief and loss is received by the victims.

When the act of giving is only done for the sake of return, it is not only a false intention, it can also cause resentment, waste of energy and unhappy relationships.

One of the automatic rewards for giving is loving to give. That's a pure, uncomplicated and enjoyable state of mind. Others can see it and feel it too.

The highest and most rewarding state of consciousness is giving to someone or organizations without their knowing it.

Giving in these ways, probably qualifies those individuals who engage in their unselfish displays of goodwill to be called "lovers." That is, one who spreads love.

How does love fit? He loves to give to her. She probably reciprocates by rewarding him. If she doesn't know it was him and doesn't reciprocate, he will probably gain comfort, confidence and peace within anyway without her returns. That is pure love within and he doesn't need outside influence to experience that kind of love. The word "probably" has been used here and will further be used in place of an absolute because, of course, no one really knows for sure what the return will be.

Giving is only half of the story. Receiving can be equally meaningful as described: She received an unselfish compliment through a male friend where "she was the best sister anyone could know." When she discovered who it was, she let him know her feelings by throwing her arms around him and hugging him tight. Returns unfold in surprising manners.

What happened was he liked her so much where, in this case, he expressed himself with a statement of love. She, in turn, was overwhelmed and returned that love in her own way.

Remaining open to receive affection is not only helpful, but it is also somewhat vulnerable which, in the case of exchanging love, makes love more profound.

The choice belongs to us all. Remain open to love, express those feelings and gain the rewards or stay inhibited and resist love by not giving or receiving and the result will probably be no or very little reward. More on opening later.

So, for someone to receive, someone must give, whatever it may be. That's a condition. Likewise, for someone to give, someone must receive. That's also a condition. It's like applying for a job. One must have something to give or the condition may be negative.

Love has it's positives and negatives. It's not all peaches and cream.

A woman won't marry a man unless he does what the marriage vows tell him ("to have and to hold in sickness and health etc., etc."). Marriage is a state of love and also very conditional.

People require similar communicative and hygienic chemistry between them to be attracted to one another. These qualities can propell them toward one another with exuberant and magnetic feelings of love. That can grow endlessly.

All these attributes may, surprisingly, be a rude awakening if the intentions are feather weight; that is, if it's only an act and not perpetrated by sincere efforts and feelings.

Since all of we humans judge in our conscious time to protect ourselves, it seems fair to say we live a constant decision making existence with like, dislike, love and hate. There are so many conditions we need to arrive at. It also seems fair to say there are conditions which qualify us for loving or being loved.

This concept of love can be ejected if you like. However, you might embrace it and discover you love it.

The questions of "Do you qualify?" is not really meant to ask someone else. It is meant for the self to ask the self.

Much is learned by studying and watching other living beings and even love movies.

If I can be so nosy as to mingle in someone's relationship, I can almost feel what they are feeling and take the words out of their mouths and bounce them back so they may see and feel their act toward one another. At that point, my act of them is far more rewarding to all three of us than any scripts of psychology. If I watch a movie on lovers reuniting (my favorite kind), I most invariably experience a pool of tears down my cheek and a gratitude of being fortunate enough to feel and react in such a manner whether or not it is from a real or stage act. That's love too.

Learning about love is only part of love's scene anywhere anytime. Sharing what is learned not only manifests the experience of love, but spreads to others who are fortunate enough to remain a little in "awe" of it all by not hiding the tears.

So ask: "Self, am I qualified to love? "Do I have active feeling?" "Do I allow them to be active, or am I so worried about what people will think, I shan't express a thing?"

Again, qualifying is not a judgment from someone else; it is a statement of openness at anytime or better still, all the time. Qualifying for love, the self can say "My door is open" or "I am opening that door for the experience of fearless self-giving and the vulnerability of receiving."

The qualification of love requires a similar attitude of getting on board a roller coaster. You want some great feelings, so you get on and take your fears with you. Even with those fears, you still receive the great feelings you desired. Once you experienced it; you know you can do it again. Sure, anything can happen. Maybe loving will be it; over and over!

Love is loving and being loved. The only part the self has to be concerned about is loving. That is, take charge at the time, in being responsible for moving some of that aliveness out of the self toward something or someone else so something or someone else can be directed toward the self too. By doing that, self-respect and self-esteem are bolstered and with that support, more of the same becomes easier.

It has been said, as you know, practice makes perfect. Well, it makes it better anyway. Take a look. Do you qualify?

Chapter 3

Different Kinds Of Love

How many times have you heard or said "I love you?" Well, the term certainly has no biased preferences. It has been said by toddlers to centurions from all nations and all sects of life on planet Earth one way or another.

Do they know what they are saying? Maybe they mean "I like you so much, but that doesn't say enough, so I'll go a step further with I love you."

Maybe they mean "I need you" or "I can't live without you." How about "When you give to me, I feel better about you."

The term "love" is really very general. There are many different perceptions of that term. Here are some:

I. Instant Love.

A new rock star appears on the stage displaying a wave of flashy talents. The young girls go into a physical and emotional tailspin unleashing some very pure feelings of joy, happiness and maybe even a bit of exotic excitement, if you will. They shout and scream.

Could anyone possibly portray a more pure form of expression which could be interpreted as loving? Another example of instant love is a young girl again, spots a boy she falls for on sight only. She probably won't extend her feelings to him too much because she has been trained to be or is just naturally reserved. She can't concentrate. She can't sleep.

If the boy doesn't reciprocate, there may be no stimulation for a relationship and her strong feelings might have to be stored.

These stored feelings are a strong liking and could be called love depending on the intensity. They can be just as intense or even more as the girls screaming at the rock stars.

Elderly people also experience instant love. That is, feelings of liking, so it evolves into a feeling of love.

Older people though, have acquired a much more sophisticated manner of approach in loving someone with all their values and game playing confusion. Everyone probably does, though, have pretty much the same basic kind of feelings pertaining to strongly liking or loving someone instantly. It's an attraction, a magnetism or like a vacuum. It's difficult to avoid unless a person has gone way out of their way to block out these attractions for one reason or another.

2. Acquired Love.

Again, in reference to humans, acquired love is not an emotion of attraction particularly. It can start with being friends with someone. For instance, two people can be acquainted in a choir for a length of time not realizing their esteem for one another is building silently over the months or maybe even years. This esteem can grow into what we conventionally call love.

Another similar example, a story of which is not widely known, is where two prison inmates spent years in the same cell and became emotionally close; so close where one of them fell in love with the other (there was no definite indications of homosexuality) and when released from prison, had complications in dealing without the other man. He had acquired what has been sometimes referred to as a case of being hopelessly in love.

Where there is a progressively strong and magnetic love growing, regardless of how, it must be realized and promoted with tender loving care or it may suffer malaise and dwindle. If nourished, that kind of love can grow into a strength with future similar to that of a tree in that it keeps on growing and like a tree, without growth, it dies.

Acquired love is not limited to romance of two human beings. That's right, it belongs to all who or which exists, sits, crawls, runs, swims or flys on planet Earth. That is, every living being can love and/ or be loved like people feel about their pets and like pets feel about their people.

Acquiring love can be like elephants discovering a pool of water after a long search; like the emotion readers gain after discovering their favorite character became dramatically reunited with a previous lover; like an entertainer accepting an award for a great performance; like a view of grand canyon while flying in a helicopter; like a person recovering from a back ache; like eating when hungry and sleeping when tired. There is no end to acquired love. It can appear suddenly, but usually is a process that requires a little more time for appreciating and absorbing.

3. Birth Love.

She says, "Becoming a mother wasn't easy, but I love my baby." Indubitably she does. A miracle has happened to her and she is thrilled with true feelings of possession and pride which will enrich her for many years.

Performing birth was a completely natural form of falling in love as compared to finding and/or developing love through judgment and common sense or any of the usual requisites necessary in social exposures.

Her baby is also a recipient of love. Mother will perform endless and unselfish services which actually teaches her baby what maternal love is all about and eventually stimulates other forms of love to be experienced.

Birth love is an emotion that is instinctually inherited probably in all living beings and grows partly from that instinct and partly from the family and/or social influences. Babies will learn how to return affection especially to their mother who shared it and actually taught it to their babies. The love of those babies, though, is only expressed to those of whom it trusts. That kind of love has it's boundaries. It is limited because the babies usually had one teacher. If the babies had more teachers, they would have learned to trust more people. Such is a typical upbringing of living beings through birth on planet Earth.

Birth love is clannish too. There again, probably all newly born living beings learn to love the first ones in their lives because the first ones, usually the family, loves them. That's the clan. The click. That's their first communicative love.

Sure, they also experience sleeping, eating laughing and a host of other comforts for security which could be considered loves. Why? Okay, give them those feelings mentioned and they are happy. Love is happiness. Take them away and they are unhappy. Having no love or loss of love is unhappiness. Love is happiness. Hence, happiness is love too.

We have seen and as we will see, love does appear to be very conditional at times; even birth love. Birth love does, though, possess the ingredients feeding the most lengthy kind of love to most all living beings and appears to be the most consistently dependable.

When the chips are down, so to speak, our at birth relative will most always be there when needed. It's highly questionable whether socially acquired loves will.

4. Love To Give And Receive.

She says she loves to write and send him letters and cards. He told her he's not good at it and it requires a lot of effort. She says she doesn't care because she enjoys sending them to him anyway. It makes her feel good.

He loves to receive the letters and cards, though and does expend energy in writing to her expressing his appreciation. She loves to write. He loves to receive. To outsiders, that may seem a little unfair, but maybe there is an exchange balance existing between them where they are both experiencing feelings of loving in there communicating. She is honest about her feelings of what she loves to do and he is the same.

Take the letters from her and the feedback from him and what do you have? Anxiety, doubt and unhappiness along with whatever else.

The holidays appear and almost everybody wants to do something for someone else including themselves. Dinners, parties, outings of all natures where families are loving to get together. Relationships form. The rich spend lavishly on others and the others scoop it all in like it was meant to be receiving in appreciation by just being there in their own different ways. The less affluent engage in similar activities, but of course, with less money and flare. The poor, having little money, may actually experience more love of giving because what they give may come more from their hearts than from their pocket books and the receivers may feel even closer to their hosts because it isn't the flare that is appreciated so much as it is the invitation of togetherness for compassion and fun.

The purest form of love offering among living beings, is doing something without wanting anything in return. That is, to give something in an unselfish manner is to think only of how much pleasure that act will rain on someone else.

That purest form is a high quality standard of receiving too, whether it is from a known or unknown source. Receiving it with a meaningful feeling of appreciation and continuing to follow suit by giving to others in the same manner without their knowing who gave it allows a perpetual give and receive circulation. That which goes around, comes around whether it is done for return or not. It just makes a better and happier person if it is done for no return.

There are, as you may have heard, church members, senior citizens, students and a host of others who volunteer their services to others with no pay. That's giving. In turn, they receive the experience of loving to give, learning to give and sharing themselves with others while gaining new friends to love.

All societies appreciate and admire volunteers. Some even love them. When some volunteers give their time and efforts to a cause, they love it so much, they discover difficulty in quitting.

The volunteers are not only the givers, but in some ways are also the receivers. They give willingly and receive rewards of feedback, love, self-satisfaction and various surprises. Giving is loving to give.

Capitalists give their services with an abundance of energy. Sure, they know they are giving to get paid well and they do it with exuberance. They love it and because of that, they do it well. They are giving something to the public and receiving plenty and love it.

Theoretically, communists give their services too with an assumed abundance of energy. The only difference is, they do it as a whole society and many times they do it in that manner so no one is burdened with blame when the government fails. The point is, true communists also love their system because, if the system is working and because they are doing what their system intended, they are surviving and loving to give and receive. The preceding was not intended to be construed as an endorsement of a particular party or policy; only an example of love.

The giving of the self through romance is probably the most universal form of love between living beings. Certainly none of us would be here if it weren't for those who were exercising their robust inherent tendencies to procreate.

Granted, all romances are not sexual. Some romances are the sharing of artistic abilities such as poetry and dancing to mention a couple. When shared with another, these talents are a form of giving to one another from their heart and soul while receiving similar expressions from the other.

Sharing a talent, whether it be artistic, mechanical, oral communication, hugs and kisses, playing or walking together is done with living being compassion and that's love. That's the feeling that is more than just liking to share. It's loving to share! Then, of course, the best part of receiving can be the great experience of feeling that love feeling. It stays with the giver.

5. Need Love.

Yes, I need love. You need love. We all need to experience the feeling of loving someone and being loved. Why deny it? The bottom line is we all have a long list of basic needs and love is one big part of them.

Neurotic? All living beings are neurotic in different degrees. That's part of life. So many of us, at one time or another have attempted to charade our feelings of needing love in fear we may appear weak and/or unstable for matehood or social acceptance. Bologna! The man, woman or child who expresses their need for love is saying "I am a living being with the intelligence and very alive feelings to express the sensitivities I was born with and proclaim one of those is my creator given need to love and be loved. The worst thing I can do is suppress that feeling. The best thing I can do is feel it and tell you!"

Here's an example: The man has been secure with his wife and kids for many years. The kids grew up and went out on their own. His wife lost her love for him because he didn't show affection. They secured a divorce. He became alone, lost his job and felt extremely insecure. He was dedicated and sexual enough to her; just not affectionate.

A few months later, he experienced emotional pains and couldn't seem to function normally. The breakup forced him to see his vulnerability. He asked her to come back. She said no. By now, he needs a fix. That is, he needs his woman or somebody he can love in his own way or at least have someone to care for.

This is really a typical case of relationship break-up and certainly nothing new. The man's needs caught up with him. He called and told her he loved her and she said "That's nice," but she couldn't respond. The more he offered her and talked, the more he cried "I need you. I love you."

She never saw this kind of almost desperately display of emotion and could not cope with it. It frightened her. It wasn't what she wanted. She didn't want a desperate man, just a stable affectionate man. He still didn't get it though, so he kept pursuing in his drive to reunite thereby pushing her further away. In the meantime, she found love somewhere else.

The man's needs of giving and receiving love were new to him and overwhelming to her. The woman had similar needs, but she couldn't allow them to be influenced and/or fulfilled by the emotion of fear and confusion. He wasn't aware of that.

The man's needs of love were also overwhelming him. He just needed a lengthily education through stumbling and therapy in rearranging his priorities and approach to others.

His need to love and be loved was always there. It just needed some stimulating to be really useful.

Considering everyone has a different personality makeup, it could be assumed the woman's needs were very little. Not necessarily true. Let's just say, at the time of their relationship, he wasn't supplying her with the needs she really did require.

The need to love and be loved can be a comfortably rewarding or disastrously destructive emotion.

Considering all living beings exist with basic tendencies, insects and wild animals probably experience similar emotional traumas as humans in their conquests to be contributing and meaningful subjects of their communities with, obviously, differences in approach than we humans.

Speaking of need, we could all learn a little more about the need to love and be loved. It's here to stay.

6. Deliberate Love.

Natural love is not planned. Deliberate love, generally, is premeditated, manipulative and designed to acquire something specific. Is deliberate love okay? Let's see.

The woman was either just plain "down on her luck" or very ambitious to accelerate her life's progress, so she sold her body as a sexual and/ or fictitious love object. This is a deliberate and somewhat calculated performance. The man pays her. Is it cold procedure?

The concept of love allows one to realize pay can also be considered a return love offering because after all, act or no act, two very human entities did share a tender and intimate experience with one another. They both planned it deliberately. They both gave something of themselves.

Is deliberate love valid? Is it right? Is it wrong? Is it right or wrong to give something deliberately and receive something deliberately? Could they both have liked the encounter so much just to say liking it wouldn't be enough, therefore loving it would suffice?

Just to hypothesize, if they both planned it and both enjoyed it with no pay involved, would the act be viewed the same? Sounds like deliberate love may have its virtues too.

Would a person have to be, necessarily, an obsessed glutton to get constant enjoyment from the deliberate sexual love mentioned?

The law of odds points out everything is not the same all the time. So, with the probability that constant sexual love may not be affectionately rewarding all the time, there is the possibility this deliberate form of human sharing can exist as okay in a tender and loving manner "some" of the time depending, of course, on religious beliefs.

Again, deliberate love is not all sexual. It is initiated by, possibly, all living beings of Earth in such a way that allows them to get what they want like a mate ("You are so beautiful. I love you"), keeping a job (buttering someone up: "Come over to my house for dinner once a week."), securing a business merger by marrying the executive's daughter or gaining the position of leading role in a movie to express the love of artistic ability. Also, young animals and humans perform many displays of talent of which they love so they may be accepted in their social circles.

We can also suffice to say deliberate love is manipulative (the skillful use of thought calculation to influence because we all want something) and could be interpreted as vicious and anything related to a vicious act is bad therefore it cannot be love. Possibly. Let's see.

Politicians have a profound belief of what they are promoting is proper, sound and righteously helpful for the people. They love what they are doing so much, they want you to be involved in their glory of righteousness.

If they can, they will almost force you to vote for them so you can feel as good as them about the cause.

Some of you will be hurt somehow, as result of the election, by some of their legislation.

You are better off, from the politicians viewpoint, than you were and he still loves what he did and thought he was right.

Actually, he still believes he is lovingly promoting his beliefs for "all" of you and all of you are so pleased, you must be loving what he is doing.

Was his deliberation a loving act or was it strictly a self-motivated manipulation? Maybe it's all in the eyes of the beholder. Deliberate love is probably here to stay. It brings living beings together in so many ways even with its scams.

7. Sales Love.

Everybody loves to make a sale in business; a sale of the self; a garage sale; you name it. When they don't make those sales, they're not happy. When they do, they are. When they make more sales, they are even happier. They are hooked on sales. They get accustomed to continued sales and it brings them so much security and fulfillment, they say they love it. Why not? They gave and they received. Isn't that part of what love is?

8. Patriot Love.

Ever since man began organizing governments, there has been patriotism. It even goes back to one tribe against another. Who knows, maybe ants and insects do it too.

Here is another case of thriving and pulsating glory among the participants. The glory of being strong, convictive and victorious is sometimes overwhelmingly displayed in public gatherings to express how much they are pleased with their efforts to rule, conquer or just prove how right they are. They love it and sometimes they are extravagant in showing their love to all. It's almost a romance of love to the public.

Patriot love can be viewed as an unselfish and almost pure form of love because it is mostly giving. Their is very little return love at the moments it happens other than occasional applause.

9. Love Of Work.

Is it love that keeps the world going around or is it work? Well, it sure keeps the bills paid, but what comes first?

A man goes to work usually after some kind of training to support his habits and/or desires, right?

They can be the conventional requirements of food, roof, girlfriend, family, car, beer, cigarettes, love, sex and a host of others so he keeps on working. He begins to like his work and his habits. After a while, he is hooked on them all and it becomes a way of life. He is not aware he is hooked. He says he likes his job and his habits. Whenever any one of his habits are taken away, like his job, he becomes distressed. Now, he is learning the only way he can appreciate what he had is to experience the feeling of loss and if he is lucky enough to get his job back, he not only appreciates it, but loves it.

He is learning just liking isn't enough. Loving is more profound and rewarding.

Now he realizes the value of his feelings and gives his job all his energy. He works hard and longer hours. His work becomes his way of life and he loves it.

He also loves his family. Such drive this man has with all his loves. Great, if he can handle them all. He may have to make some restitutions before he burns out his energy, ambition and carcass.

Again, what comes first? Can you have it all? The love commitment of work is admirable, but the love to love may have too high an energy tax to bear.

10. Conditional Love.

This has always been a popular subject to ponder over. It seems almost everyone wants an unconditional love, romance, friendship or business association. Example: "I can't marry him. He weighs me down with conditions. I want someone who will accept me as I am." "Every time I express my desires to her, she gets sensitive and accuses me of demands. It's almost like we can't talk anymore." "I almost hate to see my dad every day. He's like a naval officer giving me rules, rules, rules." "I try my best to set myself as a good example for my son to grow and mature. I teach him about life, good, bad, right and wrong and he seems to resist me a lot."

Those people obviously have a communication problem and are not aware life everywhere "is" contingent upon something else. In other words, life is realistically riddled with conditions. Love is no exception.

Unless someone has had the fortune to learn and accept all life and things do have conditions attached to them, they may just drift through life never realizing conditions, rules and regulations are a valid part of life and must be accepted to get along and survive with other beings. This applies especially where love is concerned, experienced or desired. Unconditional love is pure fantasy since we all (insects and animals too) judge and make decisions concerning others every day.

Unconditional love "appears" to exist in child birth relationships. Actually, adding a list of mother/child conditions on paper can reveal many and may be a surprise.

Conditional love is an acquired condition of using good judgment, patience, tolerance and understanding for molding, if you will and developing relationships through desire and choice. It must not be shunned as a negative perception. It is very positive, real and helpful in attaining desires and goals.

11. Infatuation Love:

This is a love of temporary emotions that doesn't possess much intrinsic value yet. It is only a beginning and may not progress to a meaningful and steady relationship which fulfills human wants and needs. It is commonly accepted to represent a temporary stimulation of desire based on a natural craving to mate or to satisfy a fantasy.

If the one who is infatuated triggers the other person to be infatuated and they both experience similar feelings, the possibility exists their infatuation may elevate beyond beginning stages of that infatuation. They may be compelled to pass through and finish that temporary excitement or enter a more advanced and complicated association with each other.

The description of infatuation love is usually done in reference to the very young whose energy drives originate from instinctual feelings, not so much from calculated judgment, therefore the path of progress in that area, may include the necessity of experiencing many impulsive and impetuous mistakes; hence infatuation.

Older and mature adults don't usually allow themselves the luxury and/or inconvenience of infatuated love. They have learned how to go without experiencing that emotion rather than be rejected. Know what the price is of becoming untimely pregnant or how to just plain be made of fool of. Infatuated love is not for everyone.

12. Hearing And Seeing Love.

There are many people, whether congenital or developed, who respond instantly to kind or educational words, truth or fallacy in advertisements and many other methods of communicating or corresponding with an open heart and mind and never find it bothersome.

The people with this particular personality (they "are" a big segment of society) listen and see like a sponge absorbs water. They love their openness and are usually very expressive in their response one way or another.

The love of their open minds is a virtue in one aspect because others usually experience pleasure in communicating with them. They are usually cooperative, pleasant, easy going, lovable and widely cultured because of their virtue.

However, the other aspect of virtue is where they can be extremely vulnerable to manipulators and con artists who only want their money, their love without reciprocation, their time (to be entertained for self-interest only) and the knowledge they can gain from being around them. Those who give, even if unsuspectingly, learn constantly about and how to love and be loved.

Nevertheless, the ones who are fortunate enough to live with this exciting and enjoyable ability to really see and hear what is beyond themselves can not only appreciate that gift, regardless of the ups or downs, but really love it and continue to express it. This too, is part of the exhilarating experience of loving when one gives it a chance.

Conquering fears builds strength and opens us up to wade through the wonders, confusion and adaptation of love with, of course, some rational degree of reservation for protection.

13. The Love To Rise And Shine.

It is said of a person who loves to be happy: "I have no one in my life but me, my good health, my ambitions and my desires to love which sometimes are a bore since they are not shared with others. I have a choice, though, to be happy or unhappy. I find no excitement in being sad, so I have chosen to be happy!

It all starts in the morning when I get up. I decided, upon waking up, to look out of myself into this world I live in and realize I am okay, calm and fortunate. The sun is shining even when it's cloudy. I sometimes think "it could fizzle," but it doesn't. Then I notice I feel so good going through my morning routine. I focus in on my priorities of the day in such a way that no matter what happens, I will attempt to perpetuate that feeling by looking for the good in everything else. To feel vibrantly alive the rest of the day is far better than to feel "down in the dumps." That's the choice I have. I will always love this opportunity of awakening in the morning to rise and shine for the shear love of being; especially being okay and alive."

14. Love To Hate.

Boy, who ever heard of loving to hate? Remember, love is a very strong emotion similar to that of hate and both have compelling drive behind them.

Since love has limitless possibilities and stems from the same emotion as hate, the negative emotion could utilize the energy of the positive emotion and become a loving to hate.

Hitler hated the Jewish people, obviously, with a passion. In view of the obvious atrocities he inflicted upon them, he was gaining successes in his rage to eliminate his foes. He hated them and apparently thought the world would be better off without them. The majority of the world's population disagreed with his tyrannical attitude, but that didn't change his passion to cleanse. If, at one time, he did have any conventional compassion for his fellow man, in general, it obviously changed into a love of hating; especially for the ones who were in his way. There are indications Hitler loved to hate.

Almost any success, long or short lived, right or wrong can be perpetuated by more of the same or similar successes and enjoyed to the point of loving them. If those successes stem from the emotional energy of hate, then love of hate surely can be felt.

The emotion of loving (that is, super liking) and the emotion of hating are conventionally accepted as positive and negative energies. Just to show how close love and hate really are, is positive always good? How about positively loving and positively hating? If they are both positive and have equal emotional strength, the possibility exists, if measured on an inertia scale, where that love and hate can be linked and move on the same wave length; hence, the consistently same emotion.

Remember, the theory of positive and negative is not necessarily directed toward good or bad. It simply means it takes one side to have another side, a top to have a bottom, an in for an out or a beginning to have an end and a million more similarities to say the least. Does love to hate exist? How about hate to love??

So, if love and hate "do not" appear to be compatible mates, so to speak, maybe changing that appearance would work better.

15. Love To Hurt.

This is probably about the same as love to hate, except hating is the basis for starting the momentum of hurt.

Whatever the reason, Hitler apparently developed his hate for the Jewish people before he began incarcerating them. Without that love to hate, he probably wouldn't have promoted such an ordeal that lead to complete immoral chaos.

Deliberately hurting another living being is a sadistic (negative) emotion of mind and can be akin to the emotion of enjoyment.

Enjoyment is liking. Liking is elemental for loving, loving is relative to hating and hating is elemental for hurting. Thank goodness their can be nothing worse than hurting.

The love to hurt is an emotional stimulation just as elevated as the love to hate except it is more educated to perform physical or psychological acts upon the self or others.

16. Self Love.

One of the most important and meaningful of all loves is for any living being, particularly we humans, to love the self.

"I have never been able to really love anybody or have anybody love me. I love my work, home and car, but that's about it."

Heard of this kind? Their are lots of them around. Unfortunately, they don't experience that connection with another living being mostly because of their upbringing. They were programmed, if you will, to eat, sleep, work and survive, but not share a very popular and cherished emotion called love. Yes, love and be loved.

Any living being can just exist on bare essentials like eating and sleeping etc., but to feel that self-reliant and sharing strength of self-love humans search for, they must experience some kind of affection or guidance when they are growing up, have self-esteem training when they become adults or purposely build successes of some kind. Any one or all are required to build self-esteem to become aware of not only being okay, but even better than that, being great sometimes. How about being great more of the time? For more self-esteem, how about "all" of the time?

Most of the time, a living being will only receive the affection from another when that being sends out some kind of signal or message, one way or another, expressing some form of an affection or willingness to share something.

Anyone who hasn't experienced affection of any kind is not confident of sharing because he or she simply didn't know how. They weren't taught or programmed to do it.

The bottom line is lack of confidence indicating low self-esteem. That is, it is the inability to have genuine respect and love of the self.

Most animals in the wild share affection with their young as soon as they can breath. It's natural with them and their social requirements are somewhat different than ours.

Humans don't always conduct themselves in a natural manner and of course, their offspring's many times will be lacking this much needed sense of self-love called self-esteem.

So, it isn't really selfish in the negative sense, it's just possessing a strong sense of self-value and pride that allows them to be open and confident enough to extend a kind of mutual greetings for possible nurturing or just to be happy when alone.

17. Selfish Love.

"If he gets hurt, that's his problem." "If they don't like what I think or do, that's their problem." "I've got mine and that's all that matters."

Loving the self is needed to love others with a more intense compassion, but loving the self can also become as obsession when the self gets stuck with self-interest only. That love becomes a neurosis, a form of mental abnormality sometimes equated as illness or disease. That abnormality can be partially congenital and partially developed as a result of someone else's influence and/or uncontrolled self-programming.

The more it is practiced, like anything else, the more it becomes manifested and a way of life. Others can usually detect it and point their fingers at what they refer to as a selfish person.

Any living being can be selfish and love only the self. They may engage in sexual activity for procreation or pleasure, but it is done for the self only, not with concern for the desires of others.

18. Puppy Love.

Since the terms puppies, kittens, chicks, kids etc. are used representing something very young, unknowledgeable and immature, the term "puppy," in relationship to love, expresses similar inadequacies for loving another being.

The phrase "loving another being" has strong connotations indicating some form of education or experience is needed to share such an omnipotent affection. This may be true with more polished and matured humans, but those requirements do not always apply to every other form of life on planet Earth.

Puppies are cute, cuddly and lovable, but don't really possess much ability to love others yet. They just want to play and play is more for self-satisfaction. At that age, self-satisfaction cannot easily be transformed into a sharing presentation of giving and loving. Puppy love is only a beginning.

Baby animals are, of course, good examples of puppy love. However, the term applies to all very young beings since they all pass through those lovable and sometimes annoying and irresponsible stages of life.

19. Sexual Love.

Sex is sex. There is no disputing that statement, at least not after all the demands of social and spiritual expectations are set aside.

Basically, all living beings on Earth were designed, apparently, to utilize this natural ability for procreation and/or pleasure.

The pleasure concept is certainly open for debate, since pleasure is viewed so much different by so many different beings. Most humans, at least younger ones, do it because the urge is strong and they can't refrain from it. Animals do it, uninhibitively, from number one, instinct, number two, reasons of tribal hierarchy and number three to procreate for maintaining or expanding the existence of their species.

Looking at the possibility, as mentioned previously, all living beings were created somehow with similar basic tendencies. Insects and microscopic life probably do it for similar reasons as animals and humans, but with less intellectual confusion as we understand it today. We still have much more to learn about small life psychology.

Obviously, the actual feeling of sex is one that is universal in concept and probably wouldn't be disputed any more than the statement "sex is sex." If that is a reasonable assessment from the standpoint of the majority, the majority may then agree the feelings of sex are the highest form of social/biological senses (people putting their bodies together).

Further, if this theory is accepted as being true, this enormous agreement of sexual feeling is not just a going along with or liking feeling, so it must be a super loving feeling. That settles that. Sexual love is here to stay as is.

20. Love Of God.

Loving somebody or something so inconceivably immense as what the term "God" represents, is to be overwhelmed with security of which that belief has offered in the past of time.

Wars have been fought and never seem to end over the interpretation of those three words (love of God) and how they fit into a society of living beings.

This particular article is not intended to influence anyone to believe or disbelieve in any concept concerning "God." The main reason for that is, of course, it may require excessive paperwork, years of writing and may not even make a significant amount of difference in belief.

The only meaningful viewpoint here pertaining to the love of God is where God, no matter what the interpretation, is connected with believing in "something," as compared to having no belief at all in what we are, where we came from or where we may go in life or death.

If the later is the case, there may be no sense of inspiration to do any loving or maybe anything else either.

If we believe in something or the self, there is infinite reason to be inspired and with inspiration, we can't help but like what we do. If we are doing it well and enthusiastically, the tendency is for us to really love that emotion, state of mind and activity.

God appears, conventionally, to be good. Devil appears, conventionally, to be bad. Also, the majority of humans appear to be engaged in spirituality of various natures and somewhat secure in their respective consciousness.

So, where does that leave us? That previous display or possibilities points out the only required strength and support needed for any form of belief is a commitment of loving what it is. These notes on God have changed since this book was written sixteen years ago.

21. Aggressive And Passive Love.

A young single and energetic salesman has not only a strong sex drive (Freudian theory) that needs to be satisfied by pursuing intimate contacts with almost every woman he meets through his charm and sales ability, but also must promote the sale of as many products as he can.

Sometimes this charging energy goes beyond being just assertive. To assert is to be more positive in approach. To aggress is to be more forceful in getting results.

Originally, the term aggression referred more to hostile and warlike procedures. In recent times, with the world's people speeding up, taking what they want, so to speak and leaving the rest by the wayside, the term has been used more loosely as an everyday expression indicating more of a dynamic approach.

Being assertive is to be confident and increasingly forward. Being aggressive is to be increasingly forceful.

Beside dynamic approach, aggressive now means it is more socially accepted in "getting what you want" with not as much hostile intentions as originally exercised.

Back to that young salesman. He either acquired his aggressive ability through family, friends, formal training or he may have been reared with a knack to be forcefully communicative. Whatever the reason, good sales people are effective manipulators. Whatever they promote, they thrive on their abilities to persuade. This requires determination and drive to the point where almost nothing else matters than accomplishing that sale whether it is for products, romance or whatever else. That is a type of aggressive determination in action and they do enjoy their creative endeavors so much where only saying "like" what they do is to discount the intensity and depth of their passion to sell. Therefore, the advanced stages of liking must become "loving" and in this case, aggressively loving to sell.

Actually, we all have an instinctual drive to sell. If not products or a service, it is selling the self for acceptance.

Thank goodness for some of this love to aggress. With many societies on planet Earth becoming more sophisticated, there are so many people letting their pride and inhibitions get in their way toward gaining that "right" mate, job or whatever else they might want.

If more people would aggressively love to take steps forward in communicating what their desires and aspirations are, there would be more responding people who could understand and be magnetized to that enthusiasm.

A possible resolution which may have paradoxical tendencies would be to reduce a desire and need for aggression and increase a desire and need for love.

Theoretically and at this rate of reversing progress, even assertive methods of achieving would slow down to a trickle. Then we would begin to experience a passive society; that is, one in which no one would do much of anything. Resolutions are only projections and have a need to be regulated.

The possibility exists, but is not probable, where this passive thinking could transform into an emotion of liking to be passive and who knows, maybe even living to be passive. There are plenty of signs around warning us.

All is not gloom and doom though. The love to be passive is common and always has been with unambitious living beings of all natures and of course, humans who have spent most of their lives forging ahead with life's successes or just barely hanging on and are worn to a frazzle.

There are also business ventures where the participants are not allowed to be active in the business activities. They are referred to as passive partners. If they are making money being passive partners, they may be experiencing more than just liking it. They may be passively loving it.

22. Love Of Challenge.

The very young, such as children of all ages ("Come on, let's go down the path and see what's there") to the very oldest ("Now I want to live for conquering my fears and see my family successfully run my business").

Those are examples of people looking forward to and challenging their desires to accomplish something.

Everyone challenges life; some without their being aware of it. Bored people strive to relieve their boredome. The handicapped are constantly challenging their abilities and inabilities in most admirable and sometimes dramatic ways. Students who study for a career are in a constant state of challenge. Housewives are known for carrying a heavy, but enjoyable, burden of challenge in raising their families and to cut this endless list a little short, the illegally inclined also pursue their daily antisociety methods in persistent manners because, obviously, they enjoy the proceeds.

Challenging is to take advantage of one of our birth rights to strive with limitless possibilities. Challenge knows no right or wrong. It just means to go forward and pursue.

So, since we all like to move forward in our pursuit of accomplishment, it seems fair to say experiencing progress and great satisfaction of some kind in this fine state of mind or even what might be accepted as the peak of the greatest feeling is really the love of challenge.

23. Love To Love.

You might say everyone loves to love. "I love my work. The time goes so fast." "I love her so much. She is the only one for me." "I love to go to Vegas." Everybody loves to do something. That's normal.

How about "I love my work so much, sometimes I don't want to go home." "I love her so much, it hurts." "I love to go to Vegas even if I gamble all my money."

The difference, obviously, is in the degree of love. One is a healthy and normal love. The other is somewhat of an obsession or greedy love.

Actually though, this is conventional love in action and who cares to analyze it, right? Well, by virtue of the fact you have read this far, you are analyzing. You are looking for more than just the way things appear conventionally.

So, loving something or somebody, even in it's advanced stages, doesn't really tell much about the ability in loving to love.

One has to identify with the emotion of love in order to love love. That is, one has to have, first, been exposed to being loved. Being loved is having someone show an affectionate interest. Secondly, more of similar experiences become, technically, educational programming in emotional love.

Time passes and one is fortunate enough to give and receive these most rewarding gifts. One becomes, maybe after a few unfortunate stumbles in life (overconfident with hasty mistakes, wanting the cake and eating it too etc.), more humble and appreciates all those gifts of love education. Then, awareness begins to form in the psyche and one begins to realize the quality of love within has been improving, thereby increasing in meaningful value for practical usage.

Adding to that, one might think, "Why would I let all that goodness slip away by not maintaining awareness of it when I can now really experience loving that feeling?" "So, I will continue to nourish it."

Seems okay to say loving love is to go "ape" over possessing that most rewarding emotion; love.

24. Natural Love.

This is the love of which all living beings, as we know them, have experienced and quite possibly always will.

This is the love that doesn't demand prerequisites to experience that love and no boundaries to inhibit it's growth or extension into the future.

This is the act, for the most part and regardless of how it is viewed, that initiates life into the place of living beings (birth). It is obviously, performed with pleasure (the love of, because love is the advanced stage of liking) and with no thoughts of self-deprivation.

If natural love is disputable, there may be reason to believe it is unnatural. Therefore, if natural love is indisputable, it is natural.

There is a natural tendency for all living beings to protect the ones they have highest esteem for to the point where they may kill to protect.

Natural love is one that is instinctual and has its comforts and hazards.

Without the judgment of man, natural love is not good or bad. It is basic and without expectations or changes. For a slightly different view, let's probe.

Is there really a natural love? Well if there is, there also has to be an unnatural love since everything in the universe is equal somehow and has two sides, generally.

Unnatural doesn't seem to fit when plant and animal life in this earthly environment exists and grows unassisted, as we need another view:

Sure, man has upset the balance of nature. How about before man appeared? There must have been something very natural and unnatural too.

With the assumption all life on Earth has always been natural, at least up to more recent times, there must have always been an equal part of everything of which was unnatural too.

Upsetting as that may seem, it has its virtues. It means these lingering tendencies have always been here as far as we are concerned.

Alright, it seems to be accepted where everything functioned naturally, but do we know what unnatural function is?

Everything falls into place as it was meant to be; whatever caused it to do so. We understand that and go and flow along with those assumptions. It is because of that assumption and understanding that we don't suffer anxiety or fear of it. In fact, the more we do understand, the more we elevate our senses of joy in number one appreciating, number two liking and number three loving whatever is a natural function.

Unnatural, in comparison, is a function on Earth or in the universe that either strikes us one way or another on Earth or in the universe in such a manner of which we do not understand, thereby raising our doubts and anxieties.

Anything we tend to view as unnatural is most definitely there. We just understand it enough to realize it is only a perception and not a thing doing something like grass growing out of the ground.

After all is said and done, natural "can" be loved. Unnatural probably will not. Again, that is two sides of perception just as it was meant to be.

The only maiden and natural love which has ever existed was love that was never altered. Before the event of human intellect, all was probably not deliberately changed for billions of years. In more recent time, man has changed almost everything; even love. Man has altered concepts, perceptions, ideas and feelings. Saying anything in reference to what man may term "natural love" is not particularly referring to what modern humans experience concerning that emotion.

Since modern humans have complicated that emotion through their intellectual influences, natural love may be a thing of that distant past and/or a very deceiving concept for today.

25. Romantic Love.

It may seem like it's the most popular love because it brings so many living beings together and continues, in varying degrees, as the relationships mature. It does have its drawbacks as well as its glories though, which are described in "other" loves. Let's just build a romance for now.

Romantic love is the stimulus that opens all living beings at the age humans call puberty, for mating and/or sexual purposes, generally.

It may be considered the most exciting of all social/sexual activity because it seems to satisfy a rush of emotional sensations called desires which are to feel the sensualities of being close to another being, sexual desires, desires to experience emotional security (real or false, it's there), desires to have a family and so many more.

Romantic love is not limited to sensuality. It is also a craving desire to draw, paint, sing, act, play piano, be a clown, develop beautiful bodies, go on ocean cruises or airplanes. One can love all of these and many more in a passionate manner. Passion is romance.

Romantic love is what one experiences while dancing slow with another and even alone. It is that which makes us cry when (in a movie) two lovers or even mother and daughter reunite. It can be exhilarating love of flying to the moon in a shuttle.

Freud probably would have said the feeling of romance is closely linked to the sexual energy that motivates all living desire.

Romantic love is the love that says "I am inspired with desire. I want. I want. I want.

26. Addiction Love.

The word addiction is usually associated with the habit of using chemically endured drugs to influence body/mind change of some kind. The regular use of a drug can become a habit. That habit can become a very neurotic vacuum or need. This is referred to as addiction.

All animal (as compared to plant) life on Earth is susceptible to addiction where there is an induced action, then is a reaction to it. If the action is continuous, the reaction becomes habit. If the habit cannot be resisted, it is considered to be addiction and continues.

Is loving someone or something an addiction too? How about being loved? Is that an addiction or is love so omnipotent it becomes an exception?

Since drugs, alcohol, cigarettes, chocolates, careers, cars, sports, friends, romantic relationships and family life are so popular among the worlds population, the possibility exists where hundreds of millions of people, to say the least, suffer from the advanced stages of habit called addiction.

Without awareness of those addictions, they can be actively manifesting and growing quietly and unnoticed. Addictive perception can actually present a feeling of contentment. Later, when there is a noticeable change or loss occurring in a particular life style, gross reality steps in and shouts "feel the pain" and emotional pain is definitely felt, sometimes, for long periods of time. This is referred to as withdrawals of addiction. That is when one's inner contentment falls victim to merciless reality of how the circumstances "are" as compared to how they "seemed."

The following is a story of love addiction: Steven wasn't even dry behind the ears before he departed from his mother's influence and married a young lady. He had no time for himself between being with his mother and being with his wife to experience being single. He became a dedicated husband and father. His kids moved out in their teens. A couple of years later, he and his wife had problems which led to divorce. They reunited a few times with no real success.

Why did they not stay together? Their marriage became a habitual way of life without much of the newly wed flare and when they separated, they weren't aware of it. When they reunited, the same problems were there and they separated again and again.

The habit of their relationship became an addiction and difficult to break. They didn't know how or what to do.

When they finally stayed apart, Steven became progressively more upset and lost his job and his dignity. He cried a lot and couldn't eat or sleep. He was really hooked and emotionally going down the tube, so to speak. He went to group therapy, returned to work and kept pretty busy while still miserable. His ex wife immediately remarried and missed that golden opportunity to pass through a most necessary withdrawal period to understand what happens with love addictions. She went through it years later.

Steven was separated two years while experiencing two fling type affairs he thought might be permanent so his whole system could relax again. It didn't work. His needs of a woman were so strong after being married so many years and never experiencing any single life, he didn't allow himself enough time to adjust his anxieties and programmed habits. Those two relationships broke up too partly because he just wasn't ready and partly because they weren't the right women.

After that, he was even more deeply involved with his addictions. He lost weight, couldn't sleep or eat and began shaking in cold sweats. He had to have his fix. He had a craving to love and make love to somebody; almost anybody. Sometime during his marriage, he eliminated his spiritual beliefs, therefore he had nothing or anyone to believe in; not even himself. That made his insecurities worse. His emotional stability was shaky.

New relationships continued. He couldn't be alone for very long and kept choosing the wrong women. He could have stayed alone and faced up to his neuroses that nourished his addictions.

He had the opportunity to do just that. A friend slipped him a drug at a vulnerable time in his life. It sent him into hallucinations that scared the daylight out of him. He wanted out of it, but there was no chance of that. He had to face all of his fears and he did just that, like it or not.

It was the most emotionally difficult time in his life. He did see how neurotic he really was. Seeing his neurosis helped to understand his addictions.

Shortly after that, he began studying psychology and helped others to whip their problems. Over the years, Steven reduced his addictive tendencies by understanding them better and had them under control.

The love of a person or a thing too, can evolve into a habit, become an obsession without knowing it and then an addiction.

Where does it start? Steven's love addiction started when he didn't really understand what love was all about. His mother didn't really display love and raising his own family, he did give and receive love in a limited manner; then it all disappeared. What was left was the torturous and emotional effects of addiction.

27. Relationship Love.

This is probably the most controversial love of all which has been, is or will be involved by one. "I want to be involved in a relationship." "My relationship is shaky. What should I do?" "I'm fed up with relationships."

Relationships, that is, love relationships, are wanted when we don't have them and wonderful, confusing and/or miserable when we are involved in them (not all of them).

Sometimes we want or need someone to be with just for a short while and it turns out to be a lifetime. Sometimes we think it will last a lifetime and boom, it's very short lived.

Love is the super blown up feeling of liking and we don't always have complete control over it. Maybe if we did, nothing would ever happen between sexual beings.

Whatever we do in a love relationship, we do it because we experience that great feeling of super liking and it "is" a form of being "hooked."

Staying consciously aware of being in that state of mind is one solution if there are any, of regulating that obvious addiction where all living beings are exposed to in relationships.

Relationships allow us the prerogative to either move into them for more enjoyment, fulfillment and growth or it allows us a choice to back off or out of the relationship if it is not what we want.

When one loses flexibility, it's like being lost. When that happens, it may be perfectly fine when the relationship seems constant and everlasting, but if and/or when it ends, look out! That's when emotional stability is put to a grueling test. The psycho/biological system would be, at that point, vulnerable to pain for an unwanted length of time before it settled down.

One of the biggest problems relationships have had was right at the beginning. Was it the right person?

Many people are insecure in being alone which is fairly normal. However, influenced by their anxiety, many will hastily and indiscriminately choose the wrong person. The following is an example:

Ed wasn't getting what he wanted and became less affectionate with Susan. He wouldn't terminate the relationship because of the fear of being alone, so he looked for someone else. This, of course, created problems between them. He found someone else and dropped her. His new relationship fell apart in the same manner and more of them after that.

Ed and all his women suffered because he didn't know who he was and didn't experience enough time being alone to discover what he was made up of. If he had, he would have been able to experience more friendships being alone and eventually find someone, through longer friendships that would evolve into a meaningful and longer lasting relationship.

Coming together is only one half of what is necessary for a meaningful relationship. The other half is staying together.

Since there are many different desires drawn together to form a good relationship, the strength of continuity is in question. How long will it last?

The length of the relationship will be equal only to the amount and quality of effort put into it. That means there has to be a desire and want to satisfy the needs of the self and a close, if not equal, desire and want to satisfy the needs of the "other" person too.

The romance may be fine for awhile in the beginning, but without knowing one has to give and surrender, the relationship may dwindle and expire. For anyone who has a longing to give and satisfy their mate, the odds will favor a lengthy relationship. The long term quality will exists, of course, if they both possess that longing to give, satisfy, be with, take care of one another and share affection. That is part of what love is all about. Love blooms when sharing affection.

Understanding the self, learning self-esteem and self-love too, all contributes toward a more meaningful love when it happens.

There are no magical methods to secure a love relationship, but there is definitely a secure feeling when two living beings come together for that priceless experience called love. Two must search it out.

How is one to know if the relationship is "right?" Initially, any relationship will work better when one understands the self better.

People say "I don't know what I want" or "I'm confused." Those are honest facts those individuals have stated and they have to learn to live compatibly with those contentions, until learning more.

They can "open the door" as they are learning how to understand taking chances in exercising the feelings they presently have of which eventually will allow them necessary experiences to move ahead in deciding faster and more prudently whether it's the "right" person or not.

Knowing whether it's the "right" person or not is only part of the equation to get the answer on moving ahead.

Proceeding and blending into a love type relationship requires a certain degree of desire and open mindedness. With some, it will be just a desire to spark the relationship. With others, it may be a wild, passionate desire based on possibly a psychobiological craving that has been building up for some time.

Desire, in this respect, does not particularly refer to sex or romance. It can mean a strong, logical and reasoning process to have companionship or family which is based on choice, not impulse.

The most rewarding kind of relationship is where a need is fulfilled by both: Ann meets Norman for the first time at a social gathering. Her mind's eyes glitter with excitement. She thinks "This is the man I want." Ann has been a long time career person and although she has had instinctual desires for a mate, she has been too busy to "open that door" to love. Her instincts are catching up with her and she allows them to talk to her. The only thing she knows about him is he was invited to the gathering, so he must be somewhat alright. She is allowing herself a chance to experience her emotions of love. Her needs have been latent, but are now catching up with her.

Norman was divorced twice. Obviously he chose the wrong ones. They both expected more from him than he was capable of giving. Obviously again, they didn't really want "him." Now it's more important for him to know the next one really wants just "him" and not what she can get out of him. Norman has now learned to remain calm, somewhat reserved, sincere and patient while staying "open" for someone new. He has learned what he wants and what he doesn't want in a relationship. He was attracted to Ann's sincerity of efforts toward him.

Ann is aware of his sensitivities and is willing to nourish a relationship with him.

They both identified with their needs and desires in another person and were honest and straight forward about them. They hit it off and moved forward with what they both wanted; a good relationship.

They both were willing to share their honesty, openness and true expression of how they felt about each other.

Too many expectations can be destructive to a relationship. Therefore, where a more meaningful and long term relationship is desired, it more likely will happen when number one, they have needs (one who doesn't experience needs of another is self-sufficient, may be self-obsessed and may not be a good candidate), number two, they must have an honest, acquired or instinctual desire for a mate or companion and last, but not least, must have the willingness to take a chance; win or lose.

Nothing really meaningful has ever happened without putting forth some kind of effort. There are millions of people who sit or stand around waiting for someone to approach them with a gift of attention, affection and/or love. It is probably better to extend efforts and lose gaining a bag of experiences than it is to sit around waiting with a bag of nothing. That bag may deteriorate after awhile and not be able to have an experience of anything. Too late? Maybe not. Maybe it is just time to bring priorities together.

Emphasis here is on knowing what and who you want and knowing what and who the other person wants, if possible. Read the book list in back for more options.

Those who expect to have whoever whenever they want create barriers of unreasonable demands on the self and on the response from others. Reducing or eliminating those barriers altogether will "open that door" for possible connections of a humble nature.

You don't like taking chances? Get this: We all are living on a very risky planet! Anything can happen at any time. Taking chances is an integral part of our heritage. There is nothing out of place by taking a few risks now and then. Just don't overdo it.

Love relationships are like the nature of trees and plants. They must be nourished and grow or they will surely die and like trees and plants, once they are dead, there is no reviving them.

Relationships are akin to most other living being activities. They will probably be here for awhile.

Treat them with respect, affection and a consciously aware mind and they will probably treat you in a similar manner.

28. Games Of Love.

Dan works in a large insurance company office. He is attracted to Marsha in the distance and thinks "How shall I get acquainted with her? Their work doesn't require communication. He purposely walks by her to get her attention and only glances at her. He thinks she will notice him and say good morning. Ironically, she has an attraction for him too, but having been raised very conservately does a very skillful act of only looking at him when he isn't looking at her. He returns to his area somewhat dismayed, but not discouraged.

This is part of the games of love. Marsha thought Dan was being "stuck up" because he was so close to her and didn't even look at her. She also rationalized they were both about the same age, nice looking and they should be attracted to one another. That thinking is an expectation which is usually an inhibiting characteristic of possible lovers and prevents attraction.

Dan, in the meantime, must proceed in his desire to conquer (get what he wants), by changing his approach. He must seek out where she eats lunch and arrange to sit near her so they almost bump elbows.

One day, it happened. They both walked into the same restaurant at the same time. Each one was so concerned about holding the door open for the other, they almost tripped on each other.

"A golden opportunity to "break the ice," he thought. Neither one wanted to display an assumption the other was "available" for the other by sharing their real feelings, so they said "Excuse me" instead of "I've been wanting to meet you" and went in two directions.

They were both accustomed to being introduced and had to continue that programming (that game). Eventually, they were officially introduced and continued to play more social games with each other for acceptance which finally did lead to matehood. It just took a lot longer than if they had stated their feelings openly.

The games of love are nothing new. They have always been here and probably always will be. Joe took Lisa to dinner a few times. One night afterward, they kissed passionately for some time. Lisa asked "What's wrong? I feel like you are holding back." Joe replied "I don't know." Joe liked her, but he didn't love her. Lisa wanted more from him than he was willing to extend. She asked "Don't you love me?" The question was too direct for him to answer yes or no. He needed more time. She was in a hurry. He replied "You're the best and kissed her passionately while she was building a fire of doubt in herself.

Both were playing a destructive love game that may have continued for months or more if one didn't stop it from happening.

Lisa's game was to capture what she thought would be love and security and do it fast.

Joe's game was to have something similar, but he wanted to let the relationship mature for a length of time to determine if it was "right."

Later, while they talked on the phone, Lisa asked Joe if he could love someone else. Joe responded, impulsively with, "It's possible."

She took that as a rejection and hung up on him and they never talked again. Good riddance? Maybe. They were both nice people.

They both wanted to win something in their strategy of games and they did, really. It certainly wasn't a long and meaningful relationship, though. But it did "get them off the hook" with each other in more ways than one. That love game was immediately stopped when Joe said "it's possible."

Who stopped it? You figure that one.

Love games also called social games from all historically calculated sources including guesswork has always existed among all living beings regardless of species. Now, without that assumption, we all think we can acquire our basic and more advanced desires of needs and pleasures by the use of game playing with one another or more. These games simply mean jockeying around, maneuvering or manipulating to get what we want.

Some were born and/or raised with more of those either instinctual and/or skills and others require more development of those skills.

Regardless of how they sift throughout the world of living beings, the games, especially the love games, are pretty much unavoidable similarly to that of love itself.

Chapter 4

Pure, Deceptive And Victim Love

Do all living beings possess the ability to love? According to scientific studies of ancient history and the previously mentioned theoretical love capabilities evaluation, yes.

The love of humans may be a little easier to understand than that of a pollywog, unless you are a pollywog expert, but being a cell living entity, they two, experience fear, doubt, anxiety, like, dislike, so why not hate and love.

Let's assume, for now, all beings are born with the same basics. They wiggle, cry out, eat, sleep, procreate, have fun and love to participate in the activity of life. That's pure and natural.

Pure love is that of which is uncontaminated and can stand the test of time. It is precipitated by desire, sincerity, simplicity and continuity. Being uncontaminated, however, is almost like being born in a filtered test tube and staying there. Humans are certainly not that protected.

Humans consider pure love as related to honesty and trust which is a basis for love that creates contentment and results in happiness. We assume the pollywogs are all very simple and happily loving one another through life until death only because we see their constant family growth and all appears well. Too bad we don't have electronic sensors to detect what they are really saying to one another. We might learn something about them and ourselves too.

All may be okay with the pollywogs and the pure, but just remember the laws of positive and negative, up and down, in and out etc. They could indicate every wiggle of the pollywog could just as easily be an influence by social pressure to enhance and develop sharing, touching, loving and sexual relationships only for the growth and survival of the species.

Loving of life and living to love seems pure, innocent and uncomplicated. That's the positive view.

Fish, lions, birds, monkeys and other animals have also been known to wiggle, cry out, eat, sleep, procreate and have fun too. They are tender with each other, share food and play together. When they want to, they attempt to mate. When they want to, the females allow them to mate. The younger ones are playful, only because they want to, which is most of the awake time. Still sounds innocent and pure, right? Remember, they didn't have to do anything. They did what they "wanted" to do. "Want" is a preliminary step to wanting more. The tendency for all living beings is to want more. How do they get it? They get it through manipulative efforts which is the use of thought calculation to influence which is inherent in most living beings.

Animals, generally, are very communicative with one another when they want something. That loving ability comes in pretty handy when they want their way. Like us, sometimes they get it; sometimes they don't.

All those previously mentioned kinds of love in chapter three could apply to animal life too. Maybe some of you animal experts agree. In this book, though, reference is being made more to possibilities, not particularly absolutes.

These animals just mentioned and undoubtedly more too, will also be deceptive in their approach. That is, if there is something they don't like, they will plan, almost like man, to correct or eliminate it. Some of them just throw a bluff to their opponents and nothing more. Others will play the show like humans of getting close, striking a death blow and possibly canabolizing; more or less.

While they jockey around, they appear aloof like it's just a day of love and play. Animals become disturbed real easily though, especially when they are hungry. They can pretend like all is normal and spring instantly on their enemy or prey.

Animals appear to be fully capable of sharing love in similar manners as humans and equally capable of deceiving their counterparts anywhere from hierarchy hostility and territorial genocide to what appears innocently killing for food.

Animal life purity appears similar to humans. It's just acted upon more instinctively.

Now, let's look at both human purity and deception. "I want to love you and be with you, but I find I need to love others too. You can love others in different ways, you know," says Jenny.

That form of romantic love is also practiced and may seem really innocent in the eyes of the beholder. However, if there is hanky panky going on, this can be not only more deceptive, but destructive to a relationship and may be more to one than the other.

Jenny's boyfriend would have to be one of those very vulnerable, pure, trusting and/or naïve types to go along with her mood or attitude, if you will.

Previous to the nineteen eighties, it might not have been a potential problem. She could have just have had the need to pass through some stages, then settle for him. But now, with the HIV threat, his situation is very risky.

She stated her love, in such a way, that he could have interpreted "others" to mean nonsexual. If he did, he was a pure lover. If she had other sexual lovers, she was a deceptive lover and he could become a victim lover and obviously, suffer serious emotional and possibly "other" consequences.

If she was straight with him, he could, depending on his personality and emotional stability, choose to be patient and "wait it out" with the possibility she may just be going through a stage of testing her own values.

Who knows, maybe she was really innocent of those sexual possibilities and they lived happily ever after. Whatever, there have been worse scenario ideosyncratical relationships.

Having more intellectual alternatives, humans have more resources to draw upon in getting what they want. They are probably nature's most cunning and loving manipulators.

We all want something most of the time. For instance, how many times have you answered the phone and you thought the caller was offering you something? How many times have you called someone with the intention of giving something with no return?

Most of the time, we call someone because we want something, even if it's "just to talk." We rationalize we are doing someone a favor by calling. Actually, we called the other person for, number one, self-satisfaction and number two, consideration for the other person. This is mild deception in action.

Let's say someone called and wanted some form of love or affection, but didn't know how to express that desire in an acceptable manner and presented one story of manipulation after another thinking one might work. This is more advanced deception which is, generally, an act of insincerely or ignorantly misleading another person. If the called person falls into some kind of relationship "trap" based on deception that doesn't work, that called person may be referred to as the "victim" of deception.

Most of the time, animals reveal their act in obtaining what they want quite readily, but humans are a little slower, sometimes by days, weeks or months because of having to respond to expectations of others.

Humans utilize a kind of sweet and sour blend of love potion called charm. They also have an ability to display a sincere, sexy and innocent appearance that influences others of whom they have an affinity or desire for.

Humans, with all their uncanny and shrewd approaches to impress others, can deprive themselves of friends, business acquaintances and/or lovers in such a frustrating and even dramatic manner simply because they may be using too much logic (their own) in evaluating their approach strategy. They are not relaxing and can complicate the strategy.

Much later, when they finally do rise above these barriers and begin communicating, they are often times nervous and uneasy in their proceedings.

Now, a person can like someone a lot, but how can that person advance that feeling to love when there are so many inhibiting restrictions such as the objective usage of logistical calculation and conformation of expectations (overly strict and up tight)?

This is what happens so much of the time with love. Love can be very simple as with less intellectual beings. Love can be pure and uncomplicated.

Sure, love is risky. Not nearly so much with animals. They don't think (as we interpret thinking) as much. If they lose, they just walk or swim away. Humans have to rationalize.

Animals are secure. They have no more and no less than they ever had, generally. Humans always want more.

Humans are so worried about acquiring someone where they, many times, don't even realize whether or not it's the right person. That is to say, they are not completely "in touch" with what it is they want. So to "have" that person, they may express those famous words "I love you" and catch a person who may be just as vulnerable as the one who said it.

Is instant "I love you" okay? If you say it is, then you have to take all the risks in your stride and be responsible for the outcome. It may truly be the right decision. Taking that chance with love can be a timely gain and richly rewarding.

Those of you who are not particularly impressed with impulsive type maneuvre may want to know more about the "tripping stone" or the many times mentioned deceptions of love.

Pure and uncomplicated love is great. Understanding and rising above the intellectual complications of love is most rewarding too. Let's see how and why.

"I love you." What does she mean? These are extremely powerful words. Of course, if they are said to the very wrong person, they won't have much effect, but to the one who is being "set up," it can mean she has never loved anyone and deserves to love him or she has had a romance with him for six months and it is time to start promoting a matehood or she got pregnant by him and this is grounds for saying it or she is emotionally hooked on him and it seems fitting to say it or she is scared she may lose him and thinks that will prevent the loss from happening or she has to love somebody without space between relationships and says it from one man to the next or she says it for getting married to him for his money or she says it because she can't live without him or she says it because he does her constant favors or she says it because she knows she can't have him.

This list can go on indefinitely. They can be viewed as just plain reasons, excuses or deceptions. Deceptions, of course, means "not as it seems."

"I love you" can be rationalized and accepted as is and becomes a simple statement of feeling within.

"I love you" can also be an excuse to that "If I don't, I will lose you."

Lastly, "I love you" can be an out and out attempt to deceive (cover up) any true and insecure feeling of self-doubt which could lead to self-loss which in turn, could not be tolerated.

Hence, as in this last example, the term "I love you" could be interpreted as "You had better accept that statement or I might fall apart and it will be your fault!" Going too far with this? Get ready for more.

Love is beautiful. By that statement and the fact everything needed on Earth is good, then all things good and beautiful can be loved.

Some people think smoking, drinking, doping, prostituting, speeding, overworking etc. is good too.

So, if everything we want in life can be termed "good" and we can't seem to live without them, the "good" and beautiful" could be termed as addictions, which in turn could state love is an addiction and while we are happy with love and unhappy without it, it may further substantiate the possibility of being an addiction and may be more deceptive than we realized.

Coming back to Earth again, this chapter only deals with the purity, deception and victim of love, not with love or its nature in general, so realize to be deceived or fooled by another person is only a perception of that fooled person. That is to say, it is how that one person only understands and/or sees that particular deception. Perceiving how one receives deception is that person's reality and belongs to no one else. One may need help with it.

Deceptive love: There can also be a deception in what the word deception means. Deception is accepted to indicate someone or something is not doing or being as we see or understand it to be. It is a possible misunderstanding in perception. The value of that perception lies in the context of the word. In deceptive love, it can mean:

1. If one deliberately uses another for self-gratification, that's deception.

2. If one thought he had a mutual relationship and resulted in not being mutual, then he is somewhat deceived.

3. If two people who were mentally incapable started an affair, but were unable to follow through, the deception may be there, but they are both unaware of it. Hence, very little deception.

4. If two people take the risk of one working overseas for years and doesn't return or if one says, "I want to check out this other person, so I can't be with you now," the context of the word deception won't apply. It will be obvious.

Deceptive love, perceiving it from the study of physics, is misunderstood. It doesn't have to be seen as good or bad. Let's see why.

Electricity has an incomplete circuit without a beginning and an end or a positive and a negative. A circuit is complete when there is a source of energy. That extends out through wires and goes around to the back of the energy source. Everything in the interim is called the flow of current.

This positive and negative concept is basic and applies to all movement and perception. Positive and negative are two sides or two ends. Nothing will move or be perceived without it.

The deception of love can be similar when the two beings involved completed an emotional circuit of love from one point in time to another. The two beings involved were the electricity moving between the positive and negative. To complete their circuit, they had to be there. Take them away and there would be no circuit (no connection). If they broke up, in this case, they just wouldn't be connected. Not good. Not bad. Just is.

So, when John says "I love you Ann," it seems like he is giving something to her. Indubitably, he is not.

If he said that to himself, he would be expressing a very pure form of love within for only him to know. If he can say "I love you Ann" silently to himself, he knows where he stands concerning his esteem for her. When he says it to her, though, it reflects a neurotic need (it is true we are all neurotic to some degree) for the two to either bond together somehow for whatever reasons or just keep the relationship in status quo.

All bonding for security, which is a direct result of our human neurotic nature, doesn't necessarily mean there has to be romance or sex involved because let's face it, family members also say "I love you" to one another.

All living beings, having basic makeup regardless of whether there is family, organizational, romance or sex affiliation, experience the good and the not so good in their relating with each other.

Filtering out the fallacies and deceptions in words for communicating in a meaningful manner with someone is beneficial for practicing the many choices we have in our approach.

Let others know, in a humble manner, you will only respond to words and actions having been proven to be not only sensible and close to the majority's reality as possible, but also to honesty of prevailing feelings in their display of desires, wishes and wants.

One way to be fair with ourselves and others is to realize our neuroses. Let us look into them. They are there. We were born with instinctual fears and aspirations. As time passes, we require more of everything. Those requirements, in turn, become manifested and multiply.

Accepting and working on them allows us to rearrange our anxieties, values and approaches with that exciting emotion called love whether it is giving (fulfilling someone's needs) or receiving (openness without resistance).

Chapter 5

Short And Long Lived Love

There is a sanctuary collecting pets so they don't have to be destroyed. They loan them out on a temporary basis if they can't find permanent homes for them.

People who are pet lovers and are not able to have them permanently because of a transient job or a pets prohibition apartment borrow these animals on a short term basis so they may experience their affinity for animals.

That craving for animals has the same emotional intensity as the emotion of love.

Many people have been known, in the human sense, to settle for this same temporary love. It may be they are looking for the right mate, but cannot handle being alone, so they "jump" from one person to the next. This usually happens because the one receiving all this temporary love discovers self-insecurities and breaks the relationship thinking another more suitable person may be the solution toward overcoming the insecurity problem.

Short lived love is apparently good for some, but not so good for others.

Long lived love is usually one existing between two individuals who were either married or had a very highly elevated esteem for one another while "going steady" or had communicated from a distant place by letters and/or phone or were just plain hooked on each other.

The married ones either purposely cultivated their love to make it last or it became a habit; not a bad habit.

The single ones either had to stay "on their toes" and continue to empress one another or their needs just didn't require any more than their good camaraderie and occasional visits.

The geographical apart couple may be building an esteem, if not a love, which may become even more rewarding to their feelings than the others because of their trust and accumulated desires for one another.

Long live love has it's virtues of emotional security which may be a bond of mutual attraction and affectionate compatibility.

That emotional security, with all having two sides, may be based on fear of being alone to say the least. Everything being conditional, again, that emotional security may crumble if the relationship is based on fear because, remember, Mary wants John to love her because he is attracted to her and wants her because he admires her, not because he is afraid to be alone.

Both of them are far better though, to have at least experienced what they had no matter where it went short term or long term, than to never have felt giving and receiving love at all.

There again, the fact love is not limited to living beings indicates there is a broad spectrum and potential in everyone's lives regardless of age, size, sex, handicap, financial, intellectual and/or health capabilities.

The first question that must be asked for anyone who is interested in love of any nature is "What do I want from this life of mine?" This might take some time to evaluate.

If the answer is "I don't know," that person hasn't been programmed to think much about anything dealing with feelings. That's okay though because, at that point in time, that person can start devising some choices of endless options life has to offer and love can be one of them. That love can be any kind of love.

The person who said "I don't know" has a significant opportunity to get involved with love. It can be quite easy; just "open that door" to love by becoming love conscious. Read about love. Ask questions about love. Start practicing what you preach about love. Open that door to love! Allow others to see that love in you and that of which you have learned about. Then, of course, promote it in every way you can imagine. It becomes a part of you and then becomes easier as time unfolds. Don't wait for love.

Some of you probably answered "I know what I want. It just isn't happening." Remember. There is only one person who prevents it from happening; you!

Do all the previously mentioned and be willing to extend yourself and take some chances. That's largely what this life is all about; taking chances.

The length of time to love anything or anybody and be loved too is somewhere in the area of being equal to the product of you, what you are and what efforts you put forth in extending yourself to others and/or a career, a craft, a project or any passion of desire.

Extending efforts of passion for love may seem, sometimes, like it's too much and the tendency may be to quit. It's okay to quit if it's something or someone who is not particularly liked because if you don't like something or someone, chances are you won't want to love them. Since it is the privilege of the mind to change occasionally, just be careful in making quick decisions in regards to quitting.

Generally speaking, all things in life have a way of working out, good or bad, depending on efforts applied. The only sure thing is; nothing from nothing is sure not something.

Chapter 6

Is Love Required To Live A Life?

Love, of all natures, certainly is available everywhere, all the time. Always has been. Always will be. Whether a person was raised around it, programmed for it or sought it out, it is always available.

Those statements may strongly indicate that love is purely voluntary since there seems to be an abundance of it available and accessible.

That, of course, is clearly a calculated assumption and requires further delving.

Jan and Tom have met and discovered they liked each other a lot. So, what happened next? The liking was very intense. They shared feelings, time and activities in a comfortable and exciting way and went from like to love until they realized they not only didn't want to, but emotionally couldn't be apart. This couple's relationship progressed well and eventually they became married and lived together the rest of their lives.

What held them together? Were they a good example for others to follow? Let's find out.

Mr. Williams was born to be a successful business executive. He was good at math, English and law etc. as a young man and excelled with his talents in the business world. He loved the excitement of challenge and success. He didn't care to do anything else except make his empire grow. In his advanced senior age, he was still pursuing and conquering and happy because of it. Happiness or addiction? Both? Neither?

Mary loved to party with all the flare, late hours, smoking, drinking and headaches. She was reminded by her friends and relatives to "cool it" so she wouldn't burn herself out. She said she didn't care and it was something she loved to do.

She continued her pursuit of party life until her late fifties when she became ill, broken down and very unhappy. She expired shortly after. Was she cheated? Continue on.

Most people know the story of the baby boy who was suddenly there in the jungle with no parents. What an awful place for a baby. Surely it wouldn't survive in a hot environment of insects, wild animals and no guidance or attention. The baby does survive though, to be a strong and healthy man who was found as a baby and adoped by the animals. They nurtured the baby with affection and taught him their way of eating and gave him the protection of their bodies (supposedly). The exposure and food wasn't as good as being raised by humans, but the affection given was definitely a performance of love and that's what helped the baby to survive and grow.

Well, whether the story was absolutely true or not is certainly open for correction or chastising. It does though, point out the love aspect of affection seems they are both about the same in this case almost insurmountable in helping to create for survival in a basically unfriendly world.

Back to Jan and Tom. All we really know is they loved each other in the beginning. Just because it was long lived doesn't mean it was all peaches and cream. Living together could have became just habit after awhile. If that's the case, would all that passionate affection called love be necessary to motivate the habit of being together? Many people live together just for the habit of preventing loneliness as mentioned earlier. Is that love? Maybe it isn't needed to live a life. It's easy to surmise now they could live romantically happy the rest of their lives, but is that realistic?

Mr. Williams, on the other hand, was, obviously, an eccentrically self-centered and strongly driven individual who knew what he was, what he wanted, got it and kept it. The love for himself and his business was, apparently, uncrushable and most important. Without those attributes and strengths, he probably would have been weak and passive, thereby incapable of building an empire of any kind.

His desires, cravings and addictions, in this case with his work, all rained and prevailed because of his sheer love in his endeavors to succeed.

You can put the following words in any order you want according to priority: desire, craving, addiction or love. Whichever one you state for number one is that which is required to live a life. Take your pick.

The party woman lived it up alright and most of the time she probably thought she was doing herself a favor with her affinity or "love" of that lifestyle. There were, obviously, reasons why she chose to live that way and justified them by saying, "It's all fun, socially satisfying and positive" or something of that nature. She also justified her gregarious and potentially self-deceiving activity by stating she loved it.

Love can be so rewarding and helpful—at times. Seems as though Mary's love had an awful high price tag on it.

The story of the jungle boy reveals a unique and legendary lifestyle. The love he received certainly wasn't the conventional type we humans identify with, especially in our very young days. At least in the story, for illustrative purposes, the baby may have survived by suckling on leaves or bugs, but there is a stronger connotation the shared affection of love is what really inspired the baby to adapt and live.

If love is really that influential for inspiring one to live and is perpetuated by the same influence, the question is will that loved one become self-sufficient eventually or will that loved one always be dependent on that care and affection?

However it turned out with the jungle boy, the attention given and received would undoubtedly create a long lasting emotional bond between them and if he did leave the tribe, would probably live as compared to dying, a full life with unique and unforgettable memories which can be drawn upon for numerous, meaningful and needed occasions.

Apparently love is "needed" by those who are less capable of caring for themselves and love is not only "wanted," but "chosen" by those who are more fortunately capable of managing their lives.

Chapter 7

Loves Losses, Awards And Rewards

When Cathy likes a particular animal, lover, house, car, smoking, audience or whatever to the point of being overjoyed with it or them is when she says, "I love" it or them. When she says, "I love" something or someone, she is strongly declaring she is "right" in her contention. When Cathy is "right" about something, no one can convince her differently. She says, "I love it and I'm not giving it up."

We humans are undoubtedly more ego driven than our animal and insect etc. counterparts and being so, tend to "hang on" to whatever we believe is ours and justify the actions by saying "I love what I have."

Ironically, this love we talk about so much pertains to clans and nations too. It is not limited to living beings and their commodities. It hovers about everywhere ready to be snatched up and used as gains, awards and rewards, financially, materialistically and emotionally.

The gains and losses of loving and being loved flow through all living beings in one form or another. In judging their value, one must realize all gains are not constant and losses are to be expected just as when a ball goes upward, we know it will come down and when it goes down will probably go back up etc. The metaphor "having a ball" may apply.

Unlike a ball, life's loves consummate, hopefully, for a longer period of time.

We learn on planet Earth, generally, to like, love, be loved, gain, maintain and/or lose. The liking, which becomes loving and being loved are the gains and are the rewards for efforts. They must be maintained through value awareness and nurturing. If they are maintained, they move up in value (gain). If they are not maintained, they move down in value (loss).

A loss in love, like any other transformation or opportunity, can also become a gain. In reference to what has been called "sick" love, abandoning the maintenance of that love may become a benefit when one realizes it isn't working, fitting or rewarding. Painful changes may have to occur for better rewards.

That also applies to the love of smoking, abusive use of alcohol, overwork, gambling, sexualizing, terrorizing or ardently, zealously or destructively participating in religious, political or any other form or radical, addictive or grandiose activity.

If one purposely abandons an apparent "sick" love relationship, that which seems a loss can become a gain of love experience because experience is a way of gaining knowledge to acquire more love. The only time love ends is when the beholder says it does.

"I love the stock market." "I love making money." "I love gathering antiques." "I love to see and hear an audience applaud my performance." "I love the movie scenes where they make me cry." "I love when my daughter says "I love you Dad." "I love being a little league coach, especially when a boy approaches me with "Can I play too?" and I can respond with, "Of course."

All this love is common and experienced by any living being in any kind of language. That is, of course, if one is willing to take the chance of expressing one's feelings exuberantly, if necessary, to gain those emotional awards and rewards love has to offer.

Obviously, all living beings will view the concept of love in different avenues of perception.

Also, all this love will bear negative possibilities. The stock market may go in reverse. The money may be lost. The antiques may be stolen or not really be antiques. The audience may "boo" or not respond as expected. The movie may be dry and unimpressive. The daughter may say "I love you," but without the "dad" that was usually added. The coaches team may have been losing too much and the boy may not have wanted to play on that team.

All gains and losses have a cost as in finance and all desired, wanted and acquired. What does love cost?

They say "You can't buy love." That is too general and can be interpreted as incorrect. You not only can buy love in many ways; you do. The cost though, as you may have guessed, is not always accomplished with use of the money. Some say too, you can't go looking for love without it. True, many places you choose to go do require money and lots of it.

If you are luxury and money oriented and you desire love of which is surrounded around luxury, then spend it in the monetary scene. You may find rewarding and meaningful treats as well as anywhere else.

However, if you can't afford it and/or just don't like the idea of having to spend money for love, then look into the following possibilities:

The primary thought to be consciously aware of, as was previously mentioned, is that love is everywhere and does bear a cost of some kind. Number one is the cost of being open for love constantly. Number two, keep it simple. Don't complicate with over analyzation and manipulative game playing. Number three, share part of you; like your feelings, your talents and your humor.

Most children, teenagers and young adults are already spending that cost by just being young. They are like a sponge absorbing how to make life work for them and gain meaningful people in their lives. Love enters quite easily for the young because they are open and yes, vulnerable too.

Without being exposed to somewhat risky situations, love doesn't have an abundance of chance to infiltrate that magical spell that runs, churns and spins throughout potentially romantic living beings no matter what or how old they are.

Acquiring love seems to be more difficult as living beings get older. They go without love because they created barriers to that openness of their younger years by allowing their opinions and fears to become too self-centered and crystallized. Is that you?

Ask "Did I get out of the house more often than not and look around?" "Did I invite people into my house?" "Did I show interest in someone other than myself?" "Do I want to share and give of myself or something to another or others?" "Do I want to improve myself for someone other than my own self?" "Do I want to become more flexible in my ways?" "Am I willing to take any risks?" "Do I really want to love someone or others or do I just want to "be" loved?"

Evaluate the questions of when, where and how to find love by looking into each one along with the previous notes on youth for a resolution to those questions on when, where and how.

Also, try and keep your resentments to a minimum. That will be priceless and rewarding.

The more experience one has acquired in gaining and yes, losing love too, the more one is equipped to handle more gains and losses of love. Just like a roller coaster, it "can" be fun, but you have to stay on the machine to experience it! If need be, use the remote control and slow it down.

Regardless of anyone's emotional makeup, probably all of us living beings identify one way or another with the feelings of being emotionally hurt. You know, the pain in the guts type. It hurts because we can't have money, a job, a person, a position or a love affair to mention a few.

We hurt because there was something we had once, lost it and wanted it again. Sometimes we get it. Sometimes we lose it and never get it back. So it goes.

So many times we hurt just thinking about losing something or somebody to the point of not attempting to solve the problem with the attitude of "it's more trouble than it's worth."

Look at how many opportunities we have missed with that attitude. Sure, they probably wouldn't have all worked out, but it isn't conventionally realistic to believe they all would.

Reference is given again to the laws of physics. A ball will travel exactly the same distance down as it was thrown up. A coin will turn over exactly one half of its two sides. Breathing in requires breathing out. A flash of light in your eyes robs you of an equal amount of sight. Everything has its positives and negatives, two sides or two ends. Not good or bad; just there.

Why wouldn't love be similar assuming those examples mentioned are sufficing to say they are not necessarily good, bad or indifferent and the pains from losing love would only be one half of the total love equation? The other half, of course, was the obvious rewards love had to offer.

Love also appears in degrees of intensity. That is, some love is mild and unexciting. Therefore, when it appears it is no longer there, the cost in pain would probably be somewhat mild and mediocre. Whereas, if it was wild and vibrantly romantic, the pains suffered may range anywhere from upset stomach to panic.

Keep the awareness where love pains, even while experiencing them deeply, are not good or bad. They are just there for the time being only; just like the ball that went up. Dealing with it and practicing patience is a super healthy and natural method of growing through that stage of love. That transformation is like turning over the coin to another side and that can mean absolutely anything. That can mean unlimited opportunity while being patient.

Yes, dealing with it is where it is at! Take the bad with the good, so to speak. Flow with the punches, lose and gain. It's all part of the process and apparently, since it's nothing new, meant to be just as positive and negative. You cannot have one without the other. It "is" all part of love's gains, awards, rewards and losses too.

Chapter 8

Beautiful, Wonderful, And Bewildering Love

After all our probing into what the possibilities of love are, need we run away from it or engulf ourselves with the romance, contentment, security, glory, power or just plain self-satisfaction love has to offer?

Since, it has been stated, "Love is everywhere," what's the big deal? There is no shortage of it. All we really need to do is allow ourselves to be loved. Then we may "fall" in love on a hiking trail, in a laundry facility, a library or who knows, maybe on a job in outer space to say the least of ten billion places. From this standpoint of view, there is plenty of it around.

The only time it doesn't exist is when we don't remain open for it.

Mary says, "I don't have it any more." Poppycock! If she had it, it was part of her. She couldn't lose or give something away that was a part of her.

That's the neat part of love. One can either discover it or review it. It's all around. Just open up and let it out and let it in. Let it be set free.

Love can be very simple. It is utilized for giving and receiving around the world and very possibly, way beyond that.

Love can also be very misunderstood and bewildering. This is natural and meant to be. Go and flow with it. We will all feel the pains of love and also be caressed by love one way or another if we remain open. That too, was meant to be. Why? Because, remember, in the basics of physics and ancient yin and yang, there are always two sides of a coin, an up for a down, an in for an out etc. and a positive and negative for everything in the universe's existence.

The same is with love. You can love a tuna sandwich (positive) and not realize, by eating one every day, that love of it may diminish possibly to not liking it at all (negative).

Loving that tuna sandwich may be more rewarding and positive if it is eaten intermittently and accompanied with more of an assortment of ingredients. Stimulation, occasionally, creates variety and that is the "spice" of life and love.

When need is stronger for love, whether it is directed toward someone or something, we can "reap the harvest," so to speak, by being a little "less" greedy through the practice of shared (not forced) affection wherever appropriate with patience, understanding and tolerance; all in reasonable degrees that is.

How about an open faced sandwich? Love is better when it's open too.

Back to Mary again. She thought she didn't have it any more. It doesn't matter how young, old or whatever titles may be placed on living beings, love has only the boundaries individuals place in front or around them. Mary placed one.

She can remove it, at least in the beginning, by removing her negative claim of "I don't have it any more" and stating to herself or maybe even shouting on the rooftop to the world "I have it and never lost it." Then she will gain steady confidence moving in the positive direction into openness.

That openness is inconceivably big and encompasses love which, in turn, allows her inconceivably big possibilities. It does allow her, yes, without strenuous effort, an inherent "power," if you will, to love and be loved. It would behoove her to remember though, as in positive and negative, yin and yang, she can't have one without the other. It doesn't work. She must extend and give something of herself to receive anything. The result may be material, a service, admiration, acceptance, liking or maybe even a beginning of love. The risks are there too. That's part of the flowing through positive and negative influences. They must not be ignored.

Are you like Mary and think you can't? If you are, let loose of those inhibitions and fears. Do something that works! Work at it. You may be pleasantly surprised to find yourself floating on a cloud while being involved.

Ho! You say you are scared to get involved? By the way, remember, this love business doesn't just pertain to living beings. It can also mean loving a job, a career, a profession, a building, musical instruments or anything else that is beyond the self.

If you are scared you might become addicted to someone or something in some way, just ask "Am I perfectly happy without love? Would I be more happy with love?

If you decide to choose the love route, the odds are more on your side for gaining more rewards when you keep your expectations of love down rather than up. Part of those rewards will be experiencing more finely controlled emotional stability. That will add toward enriching and reducing anxiety in your love affair, whatever it may be and may improve the quality.

Reading these thoughts, ideas and expressions on love, you the reader and I, the author, have been searching for a little more knowledge of this subject to possibly enjoy and share one of life's most cherished and exciting experiences.

I found, as I was writing, what I wrote didn't unfold just from acquired knowledge, but was emulated on that basis by a strong desire to share as much as I could possibly think of so you may be a little more enriched with options of love. In turn I discovered, in the desire to share, I too have been profoundly loving this search we have ventured into. This excitement tells me and possibly you too, that probing into the search for love can also be rewarding just as the results of love itself.

Also, the more I learn while writing to you on this subject, the more I realize there is so much more to learn about love.

Maintaining a pleasant course in love is remembering to be aware love is great when it is in the foreground, but it may not always be so great. People walk out and people die which means, of course, love won't necessarily be there for everyone all the time. We can all lessen the fear of that happening by learning more how to love ourselves as well as others.

Self-improvement is great, but let's not overdo it. Striving for perfection may not be needed at all. Just look at a pretzel. It's crooked, but it's "perfectly" crooked just the way it is.

Let us realize, while we briefly summarize, everyone is born with an intrinsic ability to love. Loving someone or something cannot be escaped.

Sexuality for procreation purposes is justified as basic to produce life. Life will not occur without someone loving a feeling. Sexuality is a feeling. It is an expression of desire and varies in its display from the very young to the very old. That display is like "See me, I am here, I am alive, see what I can do." Sexuality varies from the actual basic sexual act to the compassion of "let me love" to "let me be loved."

The male loves his masculinity; the female loves her femininity. They join in the love of loving. Their perception of love varies with age, desire, ambition, creativity, belief, culture, intensity, amount and many other factors, but after all their differences, they are exercising their inherent and intrinsic abilities to love whoever and whatever and are all susceptible to highs of coherent excitement and also lows of degenerate dispersion.

The crave to have someone or something is dominant and in many cases, ruling. This is where that craving can turn the overwhelming emotion of love and caring into the emotion of hate and desperation in varying degrees thereby creating the insecure feeling of doubt, mistrust and misunderstanding.

Love exists with all in a latent or outwardly form and is expressed in degrees of intensity. That intensity is why love is difficult to cope with at times. The question is whether that expressed emotion is intentionally provoked by virtue of manipulation for gaining control or whether it is just genetically inherent and is the some total of many generations' tendencies? Furthermore, is it necessary to know all that? It all helps.

Understanding love is an ongoing journey of searching for a common denominator of that intrinsic ability to love which helps to calm the confusion and deception of love.

Total understanding is an inconceivable perception. Striving for it with patience and tolerance is a healthy growth for life. That's about the best we can do.

Many times it has been said, as you may have heard, love can pop up when you least expect it. However, you must be open for it. That means you were aware it popped up because you were open to see it. If you weren't open, you wouldn't have known it popped up and may have passed right by it and missed a lifetime opportunity or at least some happiness.

Allowing some happiness with someone or something is good. Allowing more happiness with someone or something is even better. With that happiness allowance, short or longer, some beats no happiness at all.

Allow yourself to feel your love within knowing there is plenty of it available. Then, let your love out to touch others and let theirs in to touch you. Open that door to love.

Even though the words "people" and "love" are nouns, they both possess distinctly separate and specific meaning.

People are tangibles exercising endless abilities, complications and perceptions.

Love is nontangible, silent and only exists as a figment in the mind.

How expansive people seem with all their wisdom, dominance and progress.

Linguistically, love is viewed as a noun and assumed as a mere "thing" and not even measurable; especially when compared to people.

However, when perceived by love's neighbor and counterpart (people) as need or necessity, it suddenly becomes immeasurably large and important.

Did the language originators and lexicographers do justice to an obvious catalyst of human coherency?

Friendship is accepting another.

Having a friend is to take a chance.

Being a friend is to allow that friend to be.

Love is a great admiration for another.

Greatly admiring another is to exit the self.

Loving another is a gift of growth for more.

Being in love is to feel a trust for another.

Being in love is to openly give and receive.

Being in love is having "opened that door" to
the greatest feeling of all.

Lloyd E. McIlveen

Your author, Lloyd E. McIlveen unveils a chronological list of many and various book subjects presenting controversial, educational, uplifting, futuristic, self-helping, philosophical, psychological, entertaining and other stimulating concepts of which are and will be displayed with brief descriptions of each book as follows:

1. "Evaluating Outdated Beliefs" This is a report, viewed through the perception of your author of the evolutionary process and changes occurring in belief; especially in the area of religion and spirituality, This was designed for the benefit of broadening individual perception, perspective and viewing "another" plane of belief while revealing fallacies in theological indoctrination. This is an improved revision of the book's origin.

2. "Staying Alive On Planet Earth I" This is a psychology of health required to stabilize and

maintain better health for the benefit of living a much longer life. Source: A lifetime of study, problems, recoveries and many successes more in natural methods.

3. "Understanding Loss To Relieve The Anguish" Loss of anything involves many distractions and disrupting emotional disarray. Gaining greater understanding of these emotions offsets the misery of them and enhances optimism of confidence and support for emotional weakness before, at and during the time of loss.

4. "Understanding Preventing And Eliminating Cancer" presents new views on the wonders of natural methods for practical use.

5. "Paradox Of Progress Unfolding I" This is a tale told by a man "many" centuries into the future about an exciting, overwhelming and terrifying occurrence on planet Earth as a result of their wondrous progress around the time of 2300

A.D. Hang onto your seats! #2 is a second issue later on the list.

6. "Offsetting Climate Change And Nuclear Waste Contamination" This view of the two exposes the hazards, inevitabilities and possible solutions needed now for preventing a "too late" disaster that will affect all living beings too soon.

7. "What God Is And Is Not" This is a study of spiritual possibilities designed, not particularly to remold conventional mannerisms of belief, but to open and expand perception in the most controversial subject of mankind; the subject of God and whether mankind will or won't expand that consciousness along with all progress and growth on Earth and in the universe.

8. "Kids Of The Crick" This is a story of four old fashioned country kids setting out on a weekend adventure in their countryside of tall

grass, mountains, rivers, animals, caves and strange living beings. Sometimes, they aren't sure whether it's all real or not.

9. "Paradox Of Destiny Explained" eliminates the mysteries, facades, fantasies and deceptions of how, where, way and when we do what we do and opens new possibilities for expanding our beliefs and consciousness pertaining to this study of available options that may influence insight for growth, change or even justify present mannerisms of what may control the individual, planet Earth or the whole universe and is not zealous, fanatic or bigoted; only assertively revealing.

10. "Paradox Of Progress Unfolding 2" This book is a continued fiction story and can be considered exemplary of "major" human changes that alienated millions of people to another planet in the future. They are led by the elements of unexpected surprises of

which is par for the course with gutsy space pioneers. The first "Paradox Of Progress Unfolding I" must be read first to understand and appreciate the disproportional attitudes and positions of people on a threshold of major change and disasters upon them. This is not only a tale of travel, trials and tribulations, it is philosophically stimulating and adds toward future insightful expansion of the human species.

11. "Staying Alive On Planet Earth 2" This is an extended version of the original psychology of health for living a longer life. More knowledge allows more life.

12. "Preventing The Doom Of Mankind" This is a stimulating, vitalizing and somewhat shocking description of how mankind is "truly" faced with extinction in the "near" future due to their own faults of progress. It's very educational and needed now to help offset that inevitability

where the odds dictate we will all perish if we don't adhere to this offsetting of which "is" possible to achieve.

13. "Spiritual Transformation Of The Fourth Millennium" Old-time conventional religion is fading. New-time spirituality is on the rise. Objective realism is the prime issue here for future inclined thinking and believing.

14. "Understanding The Science Of Creative Mind" This is a study for discovering, developing and practicing a psychological powerhouse within for conquering the unconquerable, achieving the impossible or doing things no one has done all depending on, of course, the makeup and determination of the individual. This study brings out a greater potential of the individual's abilities when taken seriously. This was compiled from a lifetime of study and experience from your author.

15. "Living to 150" is a guidance program for intentions of anyone desiring a longer than longer life which is insightfully and innovatively educational for that purpose.

16. "The Act Of Getting One's Act Together" If anyone, business or nation wants to develop their stance, priorities and position in life, this is a chance for them to get their act together more than ever.

17. "Making Changes From This Point Forward" The design of this book is for the purpose of preventing repeated mistakes of unforeseen surprises due to what we weren't or aren't aware of that did, can or will happen again. It's all about gaining or rearranging change consciousness in this area.

18. "Relationships For All" This is a carefully arranged view of how relationships can function much better when initiated or guided by the experiences of many experts and your

author who have had failures and successes in their very human encounters. The experiences of more relationships result in wiser judgments and approaches to others.

19. "The We Between Us" helps us in discovering who is good for us and who is not. First it is a study in the book. Then it is a study with people of what exists in two party's minds (individuals, business or nations) when first confronted. A real time saver in evaluating possible compatibility or not between the two for anyone. It works.

20. "Passion Of Dance" This is a narrative on progress, value and guidance for the dance inclined. It's informative and inspiring with its history and recent magnetism.

21. "Open That Door" to love. This book is comprehensively all about love. It's not a storybook. It clears up the differences of love

that causes misunderstanding, suspicion and deception.

22. "Get The Spirit" This book describes controversial and somewhat intertwined conventional views of spirit, spirits and spirituality. This book untangles the "usual" views and presents a more perspective manner of living with these concepts of mind.

23. "Stories Of What They Couldn't Or Wouldn't Tell" Ages are from babies to 100 years; twenty four of them.

24. "Improving On Love And Relationships" This one is two books in one. Part one "Open That Door" is a psychology of love that enhances perspective to understand and adapt to a very popular, but deceiving, repressed and ignored emotion; love. Part two covers "Relationships For All" which elaborates on origination, different types, significance, deceptions, desires, experiences,

communication, possibilities, future and guidance of relationships. It's comprehensive and also derived from a lifetime of relationship experiences and serious study.

NOTES

NOTES

NOTES

NOTES

NOTES

www.ingramcontent.com/pod-product-compliance
Lightning Source LLC
Chambersburg PA
CBHW020507290526
45786CB00002B/504